3ᵉᵉ

Veg Out

Vegetarian Guide® to

New York City

D0166818

Other books in the series:

VegOut:
Vegetarian
Guide to
Seattle
and
Portland
$12.95
Paperback
1-58685-441-0

VegOut:
Vegetarian
Guide to
Washington D.C.
$12.95
Paperback
1-58685-471-2

VegOut:
Vegetarian
Guide to
Southern
California
$12.95
Paperback
1-58685-265-5

VegOut:
Vegetarian
Guide to
San Francisco
Bay Area
$12.95
Paperback
1-58685-383-X

VegOut:
Vegetarian
Guide to
Chicago
$12.95
Paperback
1-58685-384-8

VegOut:
Vegetarian
Guide to
Denver &
Salt Lake City
$12.95
Paperback
1-58685-389-9

Veg Out

Vegetarian Guide® to
New York City

Justin Schwartz

Gibbs Smith, Publisher
Salt Lake City

Second Edition
10 09 08 07 06   5 4 3 2 1

© 2006 Justin Schwartz

All rights reserved. No part of this book may be reproduced by
any means whatsoever without written permission from the
publisher, except brief portions quoted for purpose of review.

Published by
Gibbs Smith, Publisher
P.O. Box 667
Layton, Utah 84041

Orders: (1-800) 748-5439
www.gibbs-smith.com

Consulting editor: Toni Apgar
Cover design by Kurt Wahlner
Interior design by Frederick Schneider/Grafis
Printed and bound in Korea

Library of Congress Cataloging-in-Publication Data

Schwartz, Justin.
  Vegout : vegetarian guide to New York City / Justin
Schwartz.– 2nd ed.
      p. cm.
  Includes indexes.
  ISBN 1-4236-0081-9
  1. Vegetarian restaurants—New York (State)—New York—
Guidebooks. I. Title.

TX907.3.N72N477 2006
647.957471—dc22

                              2006005128

Contents

Foreword

Gibbs Smith, Publisher is thrilled to have the opportunity to initiate a series of vegetarian and vegan guides to major cities and regions throughout the United States and the world. Our primary goal is to have the guides be useful to consumers as they explore their own communities and travel near and far in search of the finest quality vegetarian and vegan fare.

We also hope to encourage and celebrate established vegetarian and vegan communities and to invite their exploration by many more people. Our objective is to further the pleasureable and health-giving effects of vegetarian and vegan dining.

We encourage you to use this guide and to be part of the creation of future guides in the series, as we revise and update each edition. As you discover new or established vegetarian or vegan restaurants that deserve the attention of others, please let us know. Either e-mail us at vegout@gibbs-smith.com or fill out and mail us the reply card in the back of this book. If your recommended restaurant is chosen for an upcoming edition of VegOut, we'll send you a free copy of that new edition.

Happy eating!

Acknowledgments

Thanks most of all to Ethel and Devyn for trekking all over the city for me and braving weekend subway schedule changes. You may now be the city's foremost experts on what constitutes a good saag paneer curry.

Special thanks as well to all my friends, vegetarians and carnivores, who joined me on reviews: Alexandra Grablewski, Elena Wiesenthal, Sneha Jhaveri, Jason Manuel, and Rhonda Greenstone, and especially Duane Winfield for joining me on the "great Brooklyn falafel quest."

I couldn't have come up with a list of restaurants like this one without a little assistance. One of my best sources was the "Vegan Restaurant Guide to New York City" pamphlet published by the member-supported, animal-advocacy organization Friends of Animals (see Resources). The website www.chowhound.com was another great source for restaurant recommendations, particularly the Outer Boroughs board on the New York City section of the site. Thanks to everyone for the tips and addresses. I'Qulah and Singh's are such great finds!

I'd also like to thank everyone at Gibbs Smith, Publisher, including Christopher Robbins for talking me into writing the book over dinner at Zen Palate; Suzanne Taylor for making the contract negotiations painless; Jennifer Grillone for keeping me on track with the manuscript; and Alison Einerson for her PR and marketing efforts. Special thanks to Toni Apgar for calling me about the project in the first place; I'm so glad we found another way to work together.

ABOUT THIS BOOK

It's official. You read it here first. I'm declaring New York City to be the most vegetarian-friendly city in America. Then again, with five huge boroughs to explore and subway lines snaking all over them, it could take years to discover all the Big Apple has to offer. That's where this guidebook comes to the rescue. I've done all the legwork for you. Which are the best Caribbean joints in Brooklyn? Where can you get the perfect falafel? Which raw vegan restaurants are setting new standards for creativity? And possibly the most commonly asked question among NYC vegetarians: with so many restaurants to choose from, where can you get really top-notch Indian food? Hopefully I've answered those questions and countless more.

Maybe you've tried consulting other general interest restaurant guides. That won't get you far. Vegetarian restaurant listings are typically limited to a dozen or two at best, lumped together with organic and health food restaurants. And as you probably well know, organic doesn't necessarily mean meatless. Even worse, the most popular restaurant guides are very Manhattan-centric, while Queens and Brooklyn are packed with fantastic meat-free restaurants: Indian, Caribbean, Chinese, and more. The fact is that many of the very best vegetarian spots in the city aren't even mentioned in other guidebooks. When I wrote this guide, it didn't matter if the food was served from a standing-room-only take-out joint in Brooklyn, a lunch cart in midtown, or a trendy new spot in the West Village. I tried them all. And I found some really amazing vegetarian food along the way.

The old standards are included here, of course. There was a time when New Yorkers were limited to a handful of restaurants serving up steamed veggies and blocks of fried tofu. Vegetarian food has a pretty bad reputation among carnivores, and it's easy to understand why. But times have changed. Unless you're on a highly restrictive diet for health concerns or trying to maintain the physique of a super model, you probably care about how your food tastes. So do I. This book was written with the average person in mind. In fact, this book was written for anyone who enjoys good food. Vegetarian restaurants in NYC serve some of the most creative and interesting food you'll ever try. Let the carnivores have their boneless and tasteless chicken breast. I prefer the likes of Caribbean roti with pumpkin curry, Indian malai kofta, barbecued tempeh, crispy falafel, and spicy Korean tofu casseroles. If you feel the same way, then give this book a read and try something new.

ABOUT THE FOOD RATINGS

First of all, the star rating pertains to the food only, not decor, ambiance, or service. The 4-star rating system is tough for a reviewer. There are some 2-star restaurants that I'd never eat at again, and others that I frequent regularly, like Dojo. I limited the number of 4-star reviews to just a handful of restaurants, but many of the 3-star ones, like Red Bamboo, are absolutely spectacular. Don't just go by the stars—please read the reviews. To earn a 1-star rating, the food had to be really disappointing. Some of the biggest letdowns were at very popular restaurants, many of which have been in business for decades. But if the food was tasteless (or even gross),

9

I felt obligated to say so. New Yorkers have so many great restaurants from which to choose, it seems a shame not to get out there and enjoy them. For the record, I never tried less than three dishes at any restaurant, and I often sampled four to six. Giving the worst of the lot the benefit of the doubt, I usually made second trips in hopes that the chef was just having a bad night. In some cases, the food was even worse the second time around.

CLOSINGS

It's sad to say, but there have been dozens of closings since the first edition of this guidebook. Closings aren't always a bad thing; I, for one, was glad to see Bachué gone. But my absolute favorite vegetarian restaurant, Anand Bhavan in Jackson Heights, shut down just as the first edition of the book hit bookstore shelves. I ventured out to Queens to dine there on my birthday and spotted a family standing outside the vacated space, staring up at the sign and holding my book. I was mortified, to say the least. I approached the father of the family, told him I was the writer of the book and that I'd traveled out for a birthday lunch; he got a good laugh out of my story. My thanks go out to him, and all of my fans who had to put up with so many closings in the past year or two. My best advice is to call the restaurants before you venture out to a new dining spot—the New York restaurant business is brutal, and great places shut down every day. The only good news is that Anand Bhavan was replaced by the all-vegetarian Dosa Diner, which is definitely worth a visit.

My heart nearly stopped when I went to get a falafel at Alfanoose in the Wall Street area one day and it was gone. I whined about the closing for months, until food stylist Megan Fawn Schlow discovered that Alfanoose had simply moved two blocks away. Sacred Chow also moved a few avenues east, and somehow transformed from a take-out restaurant I'd never liked into one of my new favorites, in cozy quarters to boot.

Restaurants that will be sorely missed include Dimple in Manhattan, though you can still travel out to Jackson Heights for it; Thali on Greenwich, which was replaced by a mediocre and over-priced Indian take-out spot; Govinda's, the cart on 52nd Street and Park Avenue—please write to me in care of my publisher if you know where Govinda's has gone; long-time personal favorite Veg-City Diner; the charming Herban Kitchen, which was such a great veggie date spot; Indian Café, a tragedy really, because the Upper West Side just doesn't have enough good food to offer vegetarians; Squeeze Bar in Williamsburg, my favorite juice joint and veggie hot dog spot; and Green Paradise, formerly located near Park Slope, where they produced some really exciting raw food and impossibly yummy Banana Coconut Cream Pie.

The good news is that new restaurants have been opening by the dozen as well, and I found some great spots that weren't in the first edition. Just remember to call the restaurants first, especially if you're traveling out to the boroughs.

DRAWING THE LINE

Thai, Indian, and Chinese restaurants litter the streets of New York. Almost all of them offer at least a handful, if not a dozen or more, meatless dishes. Even with more than two hundred reviews, I had to draw the line somewhere. I tried to figure out which restaurants are particularly popular with vegetarians, and which menus are the most "veggie friendly." Grouping the meatless dishes together on the menu or marking them clearly with a V for easy spotting helps. I looked for restaurants that offer vegetarian specialty dishes, not just the option of substituting tofu for meat. Still, there are dozens, if not hundreds of restaurants, that didn't make the cut. Mail in the card at the back of the book if you have suggestions for future editions.

A Few Ingredients to Watch Out For

Just in case you don't already know, there are a few popular ingredients that strict vegetarians have to watch out for. Unless a restaurant's menu is entirely meatless, you should assume that these ingredients are being used. You can ask for ingredient substitutions, but language barriers are not uncommon at many Chinese, Thai, Vietnamese, and Indian restaurants. And it's just unrealistic to expect your local take-out joint to make a substitution for you.

Stock: Chicken stock is commonly used in Chinese cooking for rich sauces. If your noodle soup tastes too good to believe, it was probably made with meat stock.

Pork: It has a way of showing up in Chinese, Vietnamese, and Korean dishes when you least expect it, especially in tofu casseroles and dim sum. Read the menu carefully and ask, if you're unsure.

Oyster Sauce: It's very common in Chinese and some Thai dishes. Vegetarian oyster sauce is available, but don't expect a restaurant to cook with it unless the menu is strictly meatless.

Fish Sauce: It goes by many names including nam pla and nuoc nam. If your Thai or Vietnamese food has a pungent fishy smell, you can be sure it was made with fish sauce. Forget about substitutions—it's a quintessential ingredient in those cuisines. It's like asking an old-fashioned Italian restaurant chef to omit the tomatoes from the pasta dishes.

And for vegans:

Ghee: Many Indian restaurants use ghee (made from butter) in place of oil, and the menu almost never says so. Only the finest restaurants will be able to make a substitution for you since curries are often made hours in advance. Skip lunch buffets altogether.

PANEER: Though it's lightly flavored and resembles tofu, paneer is cheese. It's featured in cubes and mashed up in many South Indian specialty dishes.

EGGS: Thai dishes often include scrambled egg. Don't be surprised if it's not listed on the menu as an ingredient. Most restaurants should definitely be able to omit it for you. The best restaurants will ask you in advance if you eat eggs.

HEALTH FOOD STORES

I can already imagine the e-mails from irate vegetarians asking, "Why didn't you include my local health food store? They serve great meatless sandwiches." It's no secret that Manhattan is littered with health food stores. I don't know when we all became such health nuts, but apparently New Yorkers are eating well. Either that or we drink a lot of fresh fruit and vegetable juices. Otherwise, only a handful of stores made the cut for a review in this book. LifeThyme has an extensive hot/cold buffet table, not to mention a juice bar, vegan desserts, raw foods, and more. Integral Yoga's market may serve the best-tasting food of them all, but the Lower East Side's Earthmatters is a revelation. Order a meatless meal and take a seat in their cozy café. Organic wine is available by the glass. For an overview of health food stores, see page 179.

And yes, I included Whole Foods. I'm not a fan of corporate chains, but you owe it to yourself to try their prepared food. Fill up a tray with a variety of meatless dishes, or order a more substantial meal from the refrigerated counters at the back of the store, and try to tell me that you aren't impressed. As for the rest of the health food stores and their premade veggie sandwiches and wraps, all I can say is, no thanks. Often the food is not made on the premises. (Ask the staff if you're unsure or don't believe me.) Sandwiches sit wrapped in plastic for hours and taste dry and lifeless by the time you bite into them.

If I included every place in New York with a juice bar in this book, I wouldn't have any space left for real restaurants. Juice bars just aren't special anymore. If you have a favorite juice place, enjoy it. You'll find me at Liquiteria on Second Avenue.

STREET SMARTS

Queens and Brooklyn have much to offer vegetarians. The food at many of Manhattan's best vegetarian restaurants, even when good, seems to be watered (or dumbed) down for American taste buds. In the outer boroughs, however, you're in for a more authentic cultural experience. Take Pongal, for example, one of Lexington Avenue's most popular Indian restaurants. Their food is good but mild, the restaurant is stylish, and it's packed with Caucasian diners every night of the week. Take a trip out to Dosa Hutt in southern Flushing and you're in for an entirely different experience. The decor is an afterthought at best, the amazing dosas are so spicy they'll blow the roof off your mouth, and the clientele is almost completely Indian.

I strongly recommend traveling to Queens and Brooklyn to try the best New York City has to offer. For the record, my favorite vegetarian restaurant is in Queens: Buddha Bodai (Chinese) in Flushing. Brooklyn is packed with great vegan Caribbean joints such as Imhotep's in Crown Heights and Veggie Castle in Flatbush (though I'Qulah in Jamaica, Queens, gives them both a run for their money). H.I.M. in the Bronx warrants a trip as well, but if you can't bear to cross the river, head to Harlem's Uptown Juice Bar for a terrific culinary experience.

Now for a word of caution: If you're a vegetarian freshman college student just off the bus from a farm in rural Pennsylvania or a tourist visiting from Kansas, please don't hop on the subway alone at night to get some great Caribbean food in Crown Heights or Flatbush. Seriously, don't.

I tried to mention in my reviews which restaurants are conveniently located nearby subway stations and which trips entail a bit of walking, but let's use some common sense. If you don't know your way around a neighborhood, make the trip with a group of friends. Travel during daylight hours just to be safe. Check the subway routes before you leave. Walk like you know where you're going, and don't start unfolding a map in a dicey area. Don't dress flashy or wear nice jewelry. Wear smart shoes or sneakers for walking. Leave your wallet at home, and bring just enough cash and a Metrocard to get around. Many restaurants in Queens and Brooklyn don't accept credit cards anyway, and ATMs can be few and far between.

Street-smart Manhattanites and residents of trendy neighborhoods like Park Slope and Brooklyn Heights may think I'm exaggerating. Let's put it this way: if Crown Heights is so safe, why is the chef at Caribbean Delicacy working behind bulletproof Plexiglas? He's just using common sense, and so should you. Websites like www.mapquest.com are very helpful when it comes to locating restaurants in the boroughs.

LOCATION, LOCATION, LOCATION

This is a New York City guide. Future editions will most likely expand the coverage area to include the greater tristate region. My research didn't turn up much in Staten

Island and the Bronx, but hopefully that will change for the next edition as well. Brooklyn and Queens, on the other hand, were a real treat. Many of the very best strictly vegetarian restaurants are in the outer boroughs. With just a couple of exceptions, every restaurant is accessible by subway. I tried to provide subway station information, whenever possible, to help you find your way. Unfortunately, a few restaurants in Queens were beyond the reach of the number 7 train. Oneness Fountain Heart, Dosa Hutt, and Zen Pavilion are all worth checking out, especially if you have a car or don't mind transferring to a bus at the end of the subway line.

THE REAL LITTLE INDIA?

New York City is home to three major Indian restaurant districts, not to mention countless smaller enclaves. How do they rank up?

CURRY HILL (Lexington Avenue around East 27th and East 28th Street): This is where Manhattanites in the know come for Indian food. The majority of restaurants serve strictly vegetarian, Southern Indian curries, as well as dosas and utthaphams, large crepes or pancakes with various fillings. Chennai Garden and the wildly popular Pongal are just about equal in terms of food quality, both very good, but the food is on the mild side. Curry Leaf, though not strictly vegetarian, is another winner, filled to capacity nightly. Vatan is located off the "strip," over on Third Avenue, and though the prices are very high, it's tough to argue with such great food and an all-you-can-eat buffet. Just bring your appetite to get your money's worth. Dimple, also just off the strip, is another winner, especially if you like your Indian food on the spicy side.

LITTLE INDIA (East 6th Street between First and Second Avenues): If every restaurant on the block shut down, it wouldn't be much of a loss. Tacky decor, pushy maitre d's trying to usher you in, run-of-the-mill Indian food, and limited veggie choices sum up most of them. Brick Lane Curry, on the other hand, is just too good for the neighborhood. Despite the lack of elbow room, huge crowds, and poor service, you're bound to be impressed by the out-of-the ordinary and richly flavored veggie dishes. Brick Lane puts every other Indian restaurant in the East Village to shame.

JACKSON HEIGHTS, QUEENS At least for me, the debate is over. New York City's absolute best Indian restaurant is Anand Bhavan. The depth of flavor and freshness of their curries have no equal. You also have to love the neighborhood (73rd and 74th Streets) for the food markets, sari shops, jewelry stores, and sweet shops. Make a trip when you have some time to spare. Dimple (in Curry Hill) has a branch next door to Anand Bhavan that's entirely vegetarian. It's a dive, but worth checking out. Jackson Diner is a winner for the trendy decor and the unbeatable lunch buffet.

CHINATOWN VS. CHINATOWN

Countless born-and-bred New Yorkers will give you a strange look if you ask them about New York City's "other" Chinatown, and yet Flushing, Queens, arguably offers up the best Chinese food in the Big Apple, if not anywhere in the country. The only reason it's lesser known than its lower Manhattan counterpart is because of the remote location—a long subway ride to the last stop on the number 7 train drops you off on Main Street. Everywhere you turn in Flushing are Chinese restaurants, Chinese-owned shops and markets, and Chinese people (with plenty of Indians and Koreans as well). Strolling around the area, you're bound to spot some familiar names. The fact is that some of Manhattan's favorites started out in Flushing, including the astoundingly popu-lar (though not very veggie friendly) Joe's Shanghai.

Besides location, why is Manhattan's Chinatown so much more famous? It depends on whom you're asking.

Carnivores fare well in Manhattan—among the hundreds of restaurants, only three are strictly vegetarian, and only one of those really stands out (Vegetarian Paradise 3). But for truly spectacular meatless Chinese, you have to head to Flushing and visit Buddha Bodai. Happy Buddha was another very popular vegetarian Chinese restaurant in Flushing, but they were closed for renovations at the time this book was being written. Keep your fingers crossed that they reopen soon.

A TALE OF TWO (OR THREE OR FOUR) PITAS

You could write a book just about NYC falafel joints. There are dozens in the East and West Villages alone, so let me apologize in advance for not including them all. After reviewing twenty or so, I had to bring the madness to an end. The falafel restaurants reviewed within these pages are all particularly popular, many for good reason.

There are two schools of pita philosophy. First, there is standard Middle Eastern pocket bread sold most everywhere, a little lifeless, thin, and sometimes chewy. If the turnover is high like at Mamoun's and Rainbow, your pita bread should be fresh. Then comes the Israeli-style pita. Breads are often made right on the premises (right before your eyes at Olympic) and are puffy, aromatic, and fresh. If you've never tried Israeli pita bread, you owe it to yourself to visit Azuri Café or Olympic soon. Most Israeli falafel restaurants also serve lafah-style bread. Lafah is larger and flatter, without the pocket. The falafel is placed on top of the bread and the sandwich is rolled up. It's another revelation if you've never tried it before, but you'll have to travel to Brooklyn for it, or stop by the Kwik Meal cart on weekdays only.

Alfanoose does something different entirely. Their falafel is served on a flaky, almost delicate, bread that doesn't fit either of the aforementioned varieties. If

you don't mind long lines, it's worth a try as well.
NYC's 10 Best Falafel (in alphabetical order)

1. Alfanoose (neither style)
2. Azuri Café (Israeli)
3. Hoosmoos Ali (Israeli)
4. Kwik Meal (Israeli—lafah only)
5. Mamoun's (Middle Eastern)
6. Miriam's (Israeli)
7. Moishe's (Israeli)
8. Olympic (Israeli)
9. Rainbow (Middle Eastern)
10. Taïm (Israeli)

USING THIS GUIDE

This guide is straightforward and easy to use. Each
restaurant entry has a rating for food and cost, and a
description of the atmosphere. It also includes a
review, and other pertinent information such as
hours, types of payment accepted, and alcohol avail-
ability. Food and cost rating keys are listed below.

Food in each restaurant is rated as follows:

★	Fair
★★	Good
★★★	Excellent
★★★★	Outstanding

Cost for each restaurant is rated as follows:

$	Inexpensive (under $10)
$$	Moderate ($10 to $20)
$$$	Expensive ($21 and above)

The cost includes the price for an entrée, plus one
drink and tip.

For the purposes of this guide, *vegetarian* means food
that is prepared without any meat products. *Vegan*

means food prepared without meat or dairy products. A note at the bottom of each restaurant listing indicates what kind of food is served in the restaurant. Not every restaurant in the book is strictly vegetarian. Some restaurants with full menus were also included if the vegetarian offerings were ample or if the restaurants were veggie friendly.

Restaurants

Manhattan

★★★ / $

1. Alfanoose

8 Maiden Lane (near Broadway)
New York, NY 10038
212.528.4669; www.alfanoose.com

MIDDLE EASTERN

Hours:	Mon-Sat 11:00 a.m. to 9:00 p.m.
	Closed Sun
Payment:	Cash only
Alcohol:	No
Atmosphere:	Take-out service with ample seating

Long-time favorite Alfanoose has moved to much larger
quarters, just a couple blocks south of the old Fulton
Street location. Thankfully, nothing much has changed
except that now there is plenty of seating, so you can eat
your falafel on the premises. You can expect it to be very
crowded during lunch hour, and the lines can get long.
Much of the food is made fresh to order, including frying
the falafel balls, and that kind of attention takes time.
What's all the fuss about? You've never seen pitas like this
before—large, very thin, flaky, and soft. A word of warning: when they ask if you want hot sauce, they really
mean it. Many customers request that the hot sauce be
served on the side, and you might want to do the same.
Order a side of the freshly prepared Foul Mudammas (fava
beans and chickpeas), and be sure to try the Mojadara
(cracked wheat), particularly the tomato and red pepper
variety. Sandwiches and platters from $5 to $9.

**FULL MENU WITH VEGETARIAN
AND VEGAN CHOICES**

★★★ / $$

2. Angelica Kitchen

300 East 12th Street
(between First and Second Avenues)
New York, NY 1000
212.228.2909

MULTIETHNIC

Hours:	Daily 11:30 a.m. to 10:30 p.m.
Payment:	Cash only
Alcohol:	No
Atmosphere:	Stylish, casual dining with separate
	take-out entrance

With its huge windows, comfortable natural wood decor,
flowers all about, decoratively painted walls, and hanging
tapestries, a long-time East Village favorite, Angelica

Kitchen is an attractive spot for lunch or dinner with a good friend. Or you can take a seat at the community table if you're dining alone. Members of Angelica's kitchen staff obviously take great pride in their craft—plate presentation is artistic but never fussy. At most pricier vegetarian restaurants, it pays to be adventurous with your ordering. Such is the case here. The soups and salads are nice, but it's the daily seasonal specials that really stand out. Fortunately the food is more than good enough to make up for the quirky waitservice. Note that the menu pricing varies widely, and they only accept cash. If you're in a hurry (and on a budget), try the separate take-out entrance and order a Marinated Tofu Sandwich to go. Main dishes from $7 to $15.

VEGAN

★★ / $$
3. Angelica's

> 147 First Avenue (at East 9th Street)
> New York, NY 10003
> 212.677.1549

MULTIETHNIC

Hours:	Sun-Thu 11:30 a.m. to 10:00 p.m.
	Fri-Sat 11:30 a.m. to 11:00 p.m.
Payment:	Credit cards
Alcohol:	No
Atmosphere:	Take-out service with limited seating

Angelica's has arguably long been the best herb and spice store in New York City, but if you've never stepped inside, you may not realize they now offer an extensive selection of prepared vegan foods, all made on the premises, organic, and kosher. They offer health counseling (by appointment), so it should come as no surprise that the food here is good for you. The point is that everything tastes like healthfood. The best advice is to order a large combo plate on your first visit, try as many different items as you can, and then judge for yourself. Even if you're on a very restricted diet, Angelica's is sure to have something interesting to offer. Seasonal vegetables are abundant. Menu choices change pretty often, so just point to what interests you, but note that the salad dressings are particularly tasty. Combo plates from $8 to $15.

KOSHER VEGAN WITH RAW CHOICES

★★ / $$

4. Apple Restaurant

17 Waverly Place
(between Greene and Mercer Streets),
New York, NY 10003
212.473.8888

MULTIETHNIC

Hours:	Mon-Thu noon to 4:00 p.m.,
	5:30 p.m. to 11:00 p.m.
	Fri noon to 4:00 p.m.,
	5:30 p.m. to midnight
	Sat 10:00 a.m. to 4:00 p.m.,
	5:30 p.m. to midnight
	Sun 10:00 a.m. to 4:00 p.m.,
	5:30 p.m. to 10:00 p.m.
Payment:	Credit cards
Alcohol:	Full bar
Atmosphere:	Stylish, casual dining

Located right smack in the middle of the NYU campus, Apple has no trouble maintaining a loyal following. Though nothing about the storefront hints at this, hidden behind the bar area is a stylish, Asian-themed dining room. Trendy lighting, pillow-topped benches, and funky banquettes make this an intimate spot for a date, despite the cavernous size of the space. Menu choices are Asian-inspired as well, although there are a handful of exceptions such as the over-stuffed Vegetarian Quesadilla. Unfortunately the cooking seems as unfocused as the menu. Protein Sushi Rolls are reliable, but the BBQ Tempeh Platter is a dud. Not even the side order of mashed potatoes can save this dish. For students, the location and atmosphere can't be beat, but there are just too many far superior vegetarian restaurants in the neighborhood to warrant a second trip. Main dishes $9 to $12.

FULL MENU WITH VEGETARIAN AND VEGAN CHOICES

★★ / $$

5. Ayurveda Cafe

706 Amsterdam Avenue (at West 94th Street)
New York, NY 10025
212.932.2400

INDIAN

Hours:	Daily 11:30 a.m. to 11:30 p.m.
Payment:	Credit cards
Alcohol:	No
Atmosphere:	Casual dining

If tranquility is what you're after, try the price-fix menu at Ayurveda. Hanging plants lining the windows, recessed pink lighting overhead, a running fountain, and Hindi statuettes and artwork all contribute to the relaxing environment. The waitstaff might not be much for conversation, but it won't matter. Once you've ordered an herbal tea, there's nothing else to discuss. Ayurveda doesn't have any menus to stress over. Within minutes you're presented with a silver thali tray filled with food and a basket of bread. Vegetable dishes vary from day to day, but you can expect green beans, chickpeas, potatoes, peas, and lentils. Everything is well prepared and satisfying, though the pakora, desserts, naan bread, and raita really stand out. Fixed price lunch $7 and dinner $11.

VEGETARIAN WITH VEGAN CHOICES

★★★ / $

6. Azuri Cafe

465 West 51st Street (near Tenth Avenue)
New York, NY 10019
212.262.2920

ISRAELI, MIDDLE EASTERN

Hours:	Sun-Thu 10:00 a.m. to 9:30 p.m.
	Fri 10:00 a.m. to 3:00 p.m.
	Closed Sat
Payment:	Cash only
Alcohol:	No
Atmosphere:	Counter service with limited casual seating

In the hotly contested battle for best falafel in NYC, here is another strong contender. You'll have to take a bit of a stroll because Azuri is located just off Tenth Avenue, but it's worth it. Don't worry about the decor, and consider yourself lucky if you can find a seat; this place fills up in the blink of an eye, despite the seemingly remote location. Daily soup specials are worth asking about, there are plenty of appealing vegetable turnovers in the counter case, and the fried cauliflower drizzled with tahini is addictively good; but make the trip for the falafel sandwich. Pitas are a little fluffier than you might expect, and the falafel is fried to a delightfully crunchy texture. If you prefer your falafel soft, look elsewhere. Sandwiches are stuffed with pickled vegetables, a coleslaw-like topping that is leaps and bounds better than the tomato and onions served at most falafel joints. We have a winner! Sandwiches and platters from $4 to $9.

FULL KOSHER MENU WITH VEGETARIAN
AND VEGAN CHOICES

★★ / $$

7. Babycakes

248 Broome Street
(between Ludlow and Orchard Streets)
New York, NY 10002
212.677.5047; www.babycakesnyc.com

BAKERY

Hours:	Mon-Sat 10:00 a.m. to 10:00 p.m.
	Sun 10:00 a.m. to 8:00 p.m.
Payment:	Cash
Alcohol:	No
Atmosphere:	Take-out service

There is no way to review Babycakes without dwelling on the retro styling. The '50s-style pink uniforms and other clever old-fashioned touches to the decor will literally transport you to something you've only seen in photographs or old movies (depending on your age of course). Babycakes looks and feels like nothing else in New York City. Peer inside the bakery case and you won't believe these are vegan desserts. Cupcakes are topped with colorful frostings and served in a variety of flavors, in wheat-free and gluten-free (and even sugar-free) varieties, depending on your dietary needs. If you expect these cupcakes to taste just like the ones at Magnolia in the West Village, you might be disappointed, but they're totally addictive and highly recommended. As if the cupcakes aren't good enough, the vegan cookies taste even better. Desserts from $2 to $4.

VEGAN

★★ / $$$

8. Baluchi's

361 Sixth Avenue
(at Washington Place, near West 4th Street)
New York, NY 10014
212.929.0456; www.baluchis.com

INDIAN

Hours:	Daily noon to 11:00 p.m.
Payment:	Credit cards
Alcohol:	Beer and wine
Atmosphere:	Casual dining

Other locations:
  All over Manhattan; see website.

With sixteen locations and counting, there soon won't be a neighborhood in Manhattan without a Baluchi's (or two). As with any chain, the atmosphere varies from one restaurant to the next. All are casual and comfortable with Indian accents to add to the experience, but older locations would benefit from a fresh coat of paint on the walls. Vegetarians won't go hungry here. Meatless appetizers like the tangy-sweet Aloo Papri and fried vegetable Pakoras served with three dipping sauces are particularly good. Entrées including Malai Kofta or Aloo Gobi, while maybe not up to the level of New York's best, are consistently enjoyable. Where Baluchi's goes wrong is with respect to the pricing and portion sizes. Main dishes are smallish, rice and bread cost extra, and a dinner for two with drinks can easily break $50. Main dishes $11.

FULL MENU WITH VEGETARIAN AND VEGAN CHOICES

★★★ / $$

9. Bamiyan

358 Third Avenue (at East 26th Street)
New York, NY 10010
212.481.3232; www.bamiyan.com

AFGHANI

Hours:	Daily noon to 11:00 p.m.
Payment:	Credit cards
Alcohol:	Full bar
Atmosphere:	Casual dining

If you thought that Afghani food is heavy on the meat, you wouldn't be wrong. It's just that, much like Khyber Pass in the East Village, the vegetarian choices at Bamiyan are so fantastic. Ethnic decorative touches and Middle Eastern–style music contribute to the dining experience, but for real fun, try to score one of the low tables by the windows where you sit cross-legged on pillows on the floor. If you've never tried Afghani food before, you're in for a treat. You're greeted with a basket of warm flat bread. Start off with Aushak, steamed dumplings served with tangy tomato sauce and a yogurt-mint sauce, available as an appetizer or an entrée. Dal Chalow is fragrant with dill, slightly sweetened by plums, and entirely satisfying. Bamiyah Chalow, made with sautéed fresh okra, is just a little sweet and a little sour; a clever balance of flavors. Main dishes from $9.

FULL MENU WITH VEGETARIAN AND VEGAN CHOICES

★★★ / $$

10. Bay Leaf

49 West 56th Street
New York, NY 10019
212.957.1818

INDIAN

Hours:	Mon-Sat noon to 11:00 p.m.
	Sun noon to 10:00 p.m.
Payment:	Credit cards
Alcohol:	Full bar
Atmosphere:	Casual to mid-scale dining

West 56th Street is teaming with restaurants to feed midtown office workers at lunch hour. One of the decisive favorites is Bay Leaf, due in no small part to the reasonably priced (for the neighborhood) all-you-can-eat buffet. Meatless menu offerings are plentiful; there are eighteen entrée options alone, including many of the usual suspects such as Palak Paneer (cheese, spinach, and tomatoes) and Aloo Gobi (cauliflower and potatoes). Coming as a pleasant surprise though, the veggie buffet choices are not quite what you'd expect. Thick and heavy curries are absent. Instead you will find lighter offerings, including spicy salads and dishes like Chole Peshwari (chickpeas cooked with onions, tomatoes, and herbs) and Bhindi Masala (stir-fried okra). For calorie counters or anyone looking for a less-filling meal when the weather turns warm, it's a welcome change of pace. Main dishes from $6 to $11.

**FULL MENU WITH VEGETARIAN
AND VEGAN CHOICES**

★★ / $

11. Benny's Burritos

113 Greenwich Avenue (at Jane Street)
New York, NY 10014
212.727.0584

MEXICAN

Hours:	11:30 a.m. to 11:00 p.m.
Payment:	Credit cards
Alcohol:	Full bar
Atmosphere:	Casual dining with separate take-out store across the street

Other locations:
93 Avenue A (at East 6th Street), New York, NY 10009, 212.254.2054;
Benny's Burritos To Go, 112 Greenwich Avenue (at Jane Street), New York, NY 10014, 212.633.9210;

Harry's Burrito Junction, 76 West 3rd Street (at Thompson
Street), New York, NY 10012, 212.260.5588;
Harry's Burrito Junction, 241 Columbus Avenue (at West
71st Street), New York, NY 10023, 212.580.9494

Greenwich Avenue is lined with restaurants that come and
go with the latest culinary trends, but Benny's endures.
Maybe it's because of the laid-back vibe or perhaps the
speedy service. Most likely it's the oversized burritos and
affordable prices that have been packing in the customers
for so many years. As the name of the restaurant implies,
the burritos are the stars here with ample meatless choices
and vegan options as well. Soy cheese, tofu sour cream,
and whole-wheat tortillas are all available for the asking.
For a hearty and satisfying meal, try a Super Vegetarian.
Don't bother with the ho-hum tacos and enchiladas. New
York City is not known for spectacular Mexican food, and
besides the enjoyable burritos, Benny's is no exception to
the rule. Main dishes from $7 to $9.

FULL MENU WITH VEGETARIAN

AND VEGAN CHOICES

★★ / $

12. Bereket

187 East Houston Street (at Orchard Street)
New York, NY 10002
212.475.7700

MIDDLE EASTERN

Hours:	*Open 24 hours*
Payment:	*Cash only*
Alcohol:	*No*
Atmosphere:	*Counter service with casual seating*

Orchard Street may be busy with shoppers all day long, but
it's the Lower East Side's late-night bar crowd that comprises
Bereket's most loyal following. If you're strolling out of a bar
at 3 a.m. with a case of the munchies, Bereket is open and
ready to satisfy your cravings. Nobody comes here for the
atmosphere; the lines are long, and the spinach pies should
be avoided at all costs. The enjoyably crispy falafel, on the
other hand, is made fresh to order. But it's the dolma
(stuffed grape leaves) that are worth going out of your way
for. Filled with rice, raisins, peanuts, and herbs, the dolma
(available in sandwich or platter form) just has to be tasted
for yourself. If you've had stuffed grape leaves before and
been less than impressed, that's because you haven't tried
them at Bereket. Sandwiches and platters from $3 to $8.

FULL MENU WITH VEGETARIAN

AND VEGAN CHOICES

★★ / $

13. Better Burger

178 Eighth Avenue (at West 19th Street)
New York, NY 10011
212.989.6688; www.betterburgernyc.com

AMERICAN

Hours:	Mon-Thu 11:00 a.m. to midnight
	Fri-Sat 11:00 a.m. to 1:00 a.m.
Payment:	Credit cards
Alcohol:	Beer and wine
Atmosphere:	Counter service with hip,
	casual seating

Other locations:

565 Third Avenue (at East 37th Street), New York, NY
10016, 212.949.7528

Fast-food burger chains had better watch their backs. Chef Louis Lanza has opened his second Better Burger joint, with eyes on further expansion. From the size of the crowds pouring out of the super-stylish Chelsea location, New Yorkers are thankful. The menu is meat heavy, albeit organic, free-range, and hormone- and antibiotic-free, but the Soy Burger and Veggie Burger make this place a destination for vegetarians. Meatless burgers are always cooked on a separate grill, there are three soy cheeses to choose from, and toppings include organic ketchup and dairy-free Thousand Island dressing. If you enjoy a shake with your burger, try the deliciously tart and dairy-free Pomegranate-Apple Smoothie. Dinner-only menu offerings include burgers served over organic penne pasta, in a stir-fry, or atop a salad as well. Burgers from $5.

**FULL MENU WITH VEGETARIAN
AND VEGAN CHOICES**

★★★ / $$$

14. Blossom

187 Ninth Avenue (between 21st and 22nd Streets)
New York, NY 10011
212.627.1144

MULTIETHNIC

Hours:	11:30 a.m. to 10:30 p.m.
Payment:	Credit cards
Alcohol:	Wine
Atmosphere:	Stylish, mid-scale dining

If every vegetarian restaurant was as good as this Chelsea newcomer, there would be no need for guide-books like this one. Touches of dark wood and velvet make Blossom terrifically inviting and so different than many of the grungier veggie spots in town. The menu is sophisticated but comforting. Seitan Medallions are served with demi-glazed vegetables, herbed soft polenta and broccoli rabe—a variety of tastes and textures, all in harmony. If you grew up eating meat as a child or only recently turned veggie, a meal like this is going to bring back some nice memories. Just like at most creative vegetarian restaurants, you're better off avoiding anything that sounds ordinary, like the Portbello Panini; it's good but not on par with other winning dishes. You absolutely can't go wrong with the inventive appetizers though. The South Asian Lumpia and Black-Eyed Pea Cakes are delightful. Entrees from $12 to $20.

VEGAN

★★ / $

15. B. Frites

> 1675 Broadway
> (between West 52nd and West 53rd Streets)
> New York, NY 10019
> 212.767.0858

FRIES

Hours:	Tue-Sat 11:00 a.m. to 11:30 p.m.
	Sun-Mon 11:00 a.m. to 9:00 p.m.
Payment:	Cash only
Alcohol:	No
Atmosphere:	Take-out service only

With a bright and shiny chain-restaurant feel and a location near Times Square, B. Frites draws a lot of tourists. That's probably a good thing because once you've tried the greasy Belgian fries, it's unlikely you'll be back. Articles on the walls say that the owner trained at the 4-star Jean Georges, but he may as well have been a fry cook at McDonald's. Comparisons have been made to favorite Pommes Frites in the East Village. Besides a similar-sounding list of dipping sauces and paper cones for serving, midtown's B. Frites just isn't up to the same level; it looks like it belongs in a suburban mall, the service is slow and impersonal, there are no seats, and the fries are oily and over-cooked. They've added smoothies and some lunch specials like Grilled Chicken and Caesar Salad to the menu, but it doesn't change anything. If you care about your health, eat somewhere else. Fries from $4 to $7.

FULL MENU WITH VEGETARIAN
AND VEGAN CHOICES

★★ / $

16. B&H

127 Second Avenue
(between St. Marks Place and East 7th Street)
New York, NY 10003
212.505.8065

EASTERN EUROPEAN, AMERICAN

Hours:	Daily 6:30 a.m. to 4:30 a.m.
Credit cards:	No
Alcohol:	No
Atmosphere:	Diner counter and limited table seating

At first glance this place might seem like an ordinary, old-fashioned Jewish-Polish diner, offering up kasha varniskas, matzo ball soup, blintzes, pierogis, and smoked whitefish. Upon closer inspection you'll realize that the menu is packed with home-style vegetarian offerings. Daily-changing specials are posted on signs all over this uncomfortably narrow restaurant, so be sure to look around before you order. Soups are served with freshly sliced challah bread—a real treat. Everything on the menu, from Veggie Lasagna to the Vegetable Cutlet a la Parmesan, though maybe not innovative, is hearty, satisfying, and a great value. Unless the idea of cramped quarters sounds appealing to you, opting for takeout is highly recommended. Located right in the heart of the East Village and open 22 hours a day, B&H is perfect when you need some heartwarming food in a hurry. Main dishes $3 to $8.

KOSHER VEGETARIAN WITH VEGAN CHOICES AND SOME SEAFOOD

★★★ / $

17. Body & Soul

Union Square Farmers' Market
(at East 17th Street)
New York, NY

MULTIETHNIC

Hours:	Mon & Wed 8:00 a.m. to 6:00 p.m.
Payment:	Cash only
Alcohol:	No
Atmosphere:	Outdoor market stand, takeout only

Other locations:
  Saturdays: Grand Army Plaza Farmers' Market, Brooklyn

Before you stock up on fresh fruits and vegetables, stop by this unassuming and totally organic Union Square

Farmers' Market stand for some vegan treats. Your eyes will first be drawn to the naturally sweetened desserts, and who can blame you? The moist and chocolaty brownies taste too good to be dairy-free. There are wheat-free desserts as well, like the Almond-Fig Cookie. Muffins are available in a variety of flavors, including Sweet Potato or Blueberry-Poppyseed. But it's the over-sized, savory turnovers and wraps that really shine here. The Saffron-Potato Wrap offers up a surprise, with chunks of plantain hidden inside. The Spinach-Portobello Turnover filled with tofu ricotta tastes like spinach quiche in pocket form, sans the eggs and milk of course. The quality and freshness of the food is impossibly high, especially at these prices. Turnovers and wraps from $4 to $6.

VEGAN

★★ / $$

18. Bonobo's

18 East 23rd Street
(between Madison Avenue and Broadway)
New York, NY 10010
212.505.1200; www.bonobosrestaurant.com

AMERICAN

Hours:	Daily 11:00 a.m. to 9:00 p.m.
Payment:	Cash only
Alcohol:	No
Atmosphere:	Counter service with casual seating

This strictly raw, vegan eatery has turned out to be a lunch-hour hot spot for healthful minded people in the Chelsea and Flat-iron districts. The staff could win awards for their helpfulness. If you show any signs of confusion when perusing the menu options, you're bound to be offered several taste samples to help you decide what to eat. Take the staff up on the offer, because the food is tasty but unusual. Ground and chopped nuts are the secret to the food at Bonobo's, giving the "spreads" texture and richness. When dining here or at any raw restaurant, newcomers should think of it as an experiment—try a few things, and then come back to try more. The prices seem a bit high, but a lot of care and creativity goes into the food, and if you're following a very strict diet, this is one of the only places in New York where you can get such healthy food in such a hurry. Main dishes from $4 to $13.

RAW VEGAN

★★★ / $$

19. Brick Lane Curry House

306-308 East 6th Street (at Second Avenue)
New York, NY 10003
212.979.2900; www.bricklanecurryhouse.com

INDIAN

Hours:	Sun-Thu 5:30 p.m. to 11:00 p.m.
	Fri-Sat 5:30 p.m. to 1:00 a.m.
Payment:	Credit cards
Alcohol:	Wine and beer
Atmosphere:	Casual dining

It's in your best interest to be patient with the spotty service at Brick Lane Curry because the food is top-notch, well above the standards set by the Indian dives of 6th Street. Take a close look at the menu and you'll notice that, in addition to specifically vegan standards such as Aloo Gobi and Chana Masala, many of the curry dishes are available without meat. This includes the Saag (creamy pureed spinach) with a choice of paneer cheese in place of chicken or lamb. Baghara Baingan, an eggplant dish with a thick, nutty-sweet sauce, is one of the most interesting Indian dishes you'll try anywhere in town. More attention goes into the stylish presentation of the Aloo Chaat appetizer than the taste, so stick with the entrees to be safe. Just don't come here if you're in a hurry. Main dishes from $9 to $13.

**FULL MENU WITH VEGETARIAN
AND VEGAN CHOICES**

★★ / $

20. Broadway's Jerusalem 2

1375 Broadway
(between West 37th and West 38th Streets)
New York, NY 10018
212.398.1475

ISRAELI, MULTIETHNIC

Hours:	Mon-Thu 7:00 a.m. to midnight
	Fri 7:00 a.m. to 4:00 p.m.
	Sat 9:00 p.m. to midnight
	Sun 11:00 a.m. to midnight
Payment:	Credit cards
Alcohol:	No
Atmosphere:	Counter service with casual seating

Herald Square and the vicinity are a dead zone for vegetarians. Fortunately, with the exception of tuna fish, the menu at Broadway Jerusalem is entirely meatless, a nice option for office workers in the area. Long but fast-moving lines tell the story—Broadway's Jerusalem is a reliable favorite with a particularly large kosher clientele. It's not much to look at, but seating is plentiful and clean. The falafel is unfussy; you won't find the variety of toppings like those at Azuri Cafe or Olympic Pita in Brooklyn, but it's fresh and tasty. Menu choices don't end there: knishes are available in a variety of flavors, including a very tasty cheesecake-like blueberry knish. You'll also find meatless soups and Italian entrées such as Eggplant Parmagiana and Stuffed Shells. For a cheap lunch, opt for a calzone or vegetarian pizza sold by the slice. Main dishes from $3 to $6.

**KOSHER WITH MOSTLY VEGETARIAN
AND VEGAN CHOICES**

★★ / $

21. Burritoville

264 West 23rd Street
(between Seventh and Eighth Avenues)
New York, NY 10011
212.367.9844; www.burritoville.com

MEXICAN

Hours:	Sun-Fri 11:00 a.m. to midnight
	Sat 11:00 a.m. to 1:00 a.m.
Payment:	Credit cards
Alcohol:	No
Atmosphere:	Counter service with casual seating area

Other locations:
All over Manhattan; check website.

For a restaurant chain—thirteen locations and growing fast—Burritoville has a sensitive eye for all things vegetarian. Tortillas are pressed fresh daily, and everything is made using fresh, preservative-free ingredients. Manhattan isn't known for great Tex-Mex food, and most such restaurants offer meager veggie options at best. Burritoville is an exception; their vegetarian menu is substantial. For example, the vegan Mega Soy Burrito is packed with tempeh, tofu sour cream, and soy cheese. Salad wraps, quesadillas, and nachos include vegetarian options as well—you can add grilled veggies, vegetarian chorizo, tofu bacon, or meatless sloppy joe. Portions are large and offer a terrific value at $7.50 or less for just about anything on the menu. The decor varies depending on the location but is consistently clean and casual. Main dishes from $6 to $8.

**FULL MENU WITH VEGETARIAN
AND VEGAN CHOICES**

★ / $

22. Café Atlas

73 Second Avenue
(between East 4th and East 5th Streets)
New York, NY 10003
212.539.0966

MULTIETHNIC, BREAKFAST

Hours:	*Daily noon to midnight*
Payment:	*Cash only*
Alcohol:	*No*
Atmosphere:	*Take-out service with limited seating*

From the crowds spilling out of cozy Café Atlas on a Saturday afternoon, you'd think they were giving away the food for free. What exactly draws the crowds remains a bit of a mystery. Perhaps everyone is ordering the breakfast omelets, because anyone who tries one of the rubbery crepes, with your choice of fillings such as mushroom and cheese, would surely never make the mistake again. There are plenty of sandwich choices, but the dry and lifeless Unturkey Slice Sandwich should be avoided. A little mayonnaise (soy mayo for our vegan readers) or maybe some ranch dressing would go a long way towards reviving this disaster. You'd be smart to cut straight to the dessert course—vegan treats are the same as those offered at both Teany and Healthy Pleasures, not made on the premises of course, but so much better than a dairy-free dessert has any right to be. Main dishes from $4 to $7.

**FULL MENU WITH VEGETARIAN
AND VEGAN CHOICES**

★★★ / $$

23. Cafe Mingala

1393 Second Avenue
(between East 72nd and 73rd Streets)
New York, NY 10021
212.744.8008

BURMESE

Hours:	*Sun-Thu 11:30 a.m. to 11:00 p.m.*
	Fri-Sat 11:30 a.m. to midnight
Payment:	*Credit cards*
Alcohol:	*Beer and wine*
Atmosphere:	*Casual dining*

Upper East Siders desperate for somewhere to eat besides Candle Cafe will be happy to find so many meatless dishes offered at Cafe Mingala, and not your standard Chinese fare either. Burma is situated between India, China, and Thailand, so it's no surprise that the cooking is influenced by all three of those nations. Fortunately you'll be too busy enjoying the food to worry much about how to define Burmese cuisine. Several "soy protein" dishes listed in the "Special Vegetarian" section of the menu are essentially the same, varying only in the flavor of the sauce. The flavors are so good, you'll want to try them all—Mango, Lemon, Ginger, Basil, and more. Just don't skip appetizers such as the falafel-like Crispy Lentil Fritters and the Golden Fingers Tempura, battered and fried calabash squash, both served with a sweet and spicy dipping sauce. Main dishes from $8 to $11.

FULL MENU WITH VEGETARIAN
AND VEGAN CHOICES

★★★ / $$
24. Café Orlin

41 St. Marks Place
(between Second and First Avenues)
New York, NY 10009
212.477.1447

MULTIETHNIC

Hours:	*Sun-Thu 8:30 a.m. to 2:00 a.m.*
	Fri-Sat open 24 hours
Payment:	*Credit cards*
Alcohol:	*Beer and wine*
Atmosphere:	*Casual dining*

Nearly an East Village institution, Café Orlin packs in the regulars day and night. Good thing it's open twenty-four hours on Fridays and Saturdays. You're in for a wonderful surprise if you've written it off as just another overcrowded brunch spot. The meatless menu offerings really shine. Add to that the quaint café-style decor, reasonable prices, and prompt and friendly wait-service, and you have a winner. Unlike nearby cafés that serve little more than falafel for vegetarians, Café Orlin's menu includes veggie entrées, salads, sandwiches, pastas, and more. The Linguine with Rosemary-Tomato Sauce is fragrant and fresh tasting, but not heavy at all. Smothered with sautéed soy beans and mushrooms, the Soy Glazed Tofu Sandwich on toasted bread is as unique as it is satisfying. Main dishes from $7 to $10.

FULL MENU WITH VEGETARIAN
AND VEGAN CHOICES

★★ / $
25. Cafe Rakka

81 St. Mark's Place
(between First and Second Avenues)
New York, NY 10003
212.982.9166

MIDDLE EASTERN

Hours:	Daily noon to midnight
Payment:	Cash only
Alcohol:	No
Atmosphere:	Counter service with casual seating

Other locations:
38 Avenue B (between East 3rd and East 4th Streets),
New York, NY 10009, 212.777.5264

As evidenced by the constant crowds, it's obvious that
Cafe Rakka is an East Village favorite. With a prime location on St. Mark's near First Avenue and an outrageously
cheap menu, it's easy to understand why. There are
seats both indoors and out, a nice change of pace for a
Middle Eastern falafel joint in New York City, but
nobody comes here for the ambiance. If the line looks
long, remember that almost everything is prepared in
advance and heated as necessary, so you'll never have to
wait long for your order. Don't expect anything out of
the ordinary; this is the place to come for reliable
falafel, hummus, baba ghanoush, couscous, fava bean
salads, mujadarra, and tabouli, all available in sandwich
or platter form. Better yet, order a combo plate and
choose up to four different dishes. Fresh juices are available as well. Sandwiches and platters from $3 to $7.

**FULL MENU WITH VEGETARIAN
AND VEGAN CHOICES**

★★★ / $
26. Cafe Spice

72 University Place
(between East 10th and East 11th Streets)
New York, NY 10003
212.253.6999; www.cafespice.com

INDIAN

Hours:	Mon-Wed 11:30 a.m. to 10:30 p.m.
	Thu-Fri 11:30 a.m. to 11:30 p.m.
	Sat 1:00 p.m. to 11:30 p.m.
	Sun 1:00 p.m. to 10:30 p.m.
Payment:	Credit cards
Alcohol:	Full bar
Atmosphere:	Stylish, casual to mid-scale dining

Other locations:
  54 West 55th Street, New York, NY 10019, 212.489.7444;
  537 Washington Boulevard, Jersey City, NJ 07310,
    201.533-0111

Much as the nearby but unrelated restaurant Spice has done for Thai food, Cafe Spice presents Indian food in trendy, stylish surroundings. Dramatic lighting sets the mood, and attentive service completes the experience. Arrive early with a special someone, and try to score one of the intimate booths. Just don't forget the credit card, because this is some of the priciest Indian food in town. You get a lot for your money though—naan bread, dal, rice, and a vegetable side dish are included for the cost of an entrée. You will never leave unsatisfied. Nouvelle Indian is the best way to describe the food. Purists would not approve; every dish on the menu is a little sweeter or saltier or more boldly spiced than in traditional restaurants, not that that's a bad thing. From the Saag Paneer to the Goa Vegetable Curry, everything is fresh, rich, and exciting. Main dishes from $14 to $16.

**FULL MENU WITH VEGETARIAN
AND VEGAN CHOICES**

★★★ / $

27. Cafe Spice Express

*Dining Concourse, Grand Central Station,
East 42nd Street (between Madison and Lexington
Avenues)
New York, NY
646.227.1300; www.cafespice.com*

INDIAN

Hours:	*Daily 11:00 a.m. to 9:00 p.m.*
Payment:	*Credit cards*
Alcohol:	*Beer*
Atmosphere:	*Counter service with casual seating in dining concourse*

Other locations:
  Roosevelt Field Mall Food Court, Intersection at Old
    Country Road and Meadowbrook Parkway, Garden City,
    NY 11530

Grand Central Station's stunning renovation includes an all-new dining concourse with ample seating for both office workers at lunch and commuters during rush hour. Cafe Spice, a trendy nouvelle-Indian restaurant in the Village, has opened a take-out stand (hence the name "Express") with a more traditional-tasting menu. Even when judged by the toughest standards, the food is fantastic. Menu choices, at least half of which are vegetarian, change daily. Order a combination plate for the best value. The Saag Paneer (spinach and cheese) is fragrant and flavorful with a wonderful creamy but not overly pureed texture. Aloo Gobi is tangy and packed with veggies. All of the curries are a little on the spicy side, but it's nothing some rice won't cool down. Portions are huge; if you're dining with a friend, order one combo plate and the delightfully crispy potato samosas and share. Main dishes from $8 to $10.

FULL MENU WITH VEGETARIAN AND VEGAN CHOICES

★★★ / $$

28. Candle Cafe

1307 Third Avenue
(between East 74th and East 75th Streets)
New York, NY 10021
212.472.0970; www.candlecafe.com

MULTIETHNIC

Hours:	Mon-Sat 11:30 a.m. to 10:30 p.m.
	Sun 11:30 a.m. to 9:30 p.m.
Payment:	Credit cards
Alcohol:	Organic wines
Atmosphere:	Stylish, casual dining

Take a break from shopping on this fashionable strip of Third Avenue on the Upper East Side to enjoy some of the most creative vegetarian food in the city. Organic ingredients served at the peak of their season seem to be the mission at Candle Cafe. Everything about the restaurant is casual yet stylish: old hardwood floors, dark tiles around the juice bar, earth-toned fabrics adorning the walls. Whether you're on a date, dining out with a good friend, or even sitting alone at the bar, the ambiance seems just right. Just like the decor, the food here isn't pretentious at all. Vegetarian Lasagna with soy mozzarella tastes so good, you'll never miss the meat sauce. The Crystal Roll appetizer with its peanut-coconut dipping sauce is a treat. If the list of daily specials seems daunting, let the friendly waitstaff make a recommendation. But at these prices, don't forget the credit card. Main dishes from $9 to $16.

VEGAN

★★★ / $$$

29. Candle 79

154 East 79th Street (near Lexington Avenue)
New York, NY 10021
212.437.7179; www.candlecafe.com

AMERICAN, MULTIETHNIC

Hours:	Mon-Sat noon to 3:30 p.m.
	and 5:30 p.m. to 10:30 p.m.
	Sun noon to 4:00 p.m.
	and 5:00 p.m. to 10:00 p.m.
Payment:	Credit cards
Alcohol:	Wine
Atmosphere:	Stylish, mid-scale dining

Think of this as a more upscale version of the famous
Candle Café, and you won't be disappointed. It's gorgeous inside, so invite someone along for a special
night on the town. The menu at Candle 79 is also sure
to impress, and it seems to be part of a movement in
New York City to bring the mid- to upscale dining experience to ecologically-minded customers. You almost
don't need to read this review, because the food is so
thoughtfully prepared and beautifully presented, but
start off with the Grilled Setain Chimichurri and the
Crispy Dumplings if you need a recommendation. In
case your waiter doesn't mention it, the Seitan Picatta
is their signature dish. If you have any fond memories
of eating meat, this amazing dish is likely to conjure
them up, served with creamed spinach, roasted garlic
mashed potatoes, and a lemon-caper sauce that you'll
be dreaming about for days. Entrees from $18 to $23.

ORGANIC VEGETARIAN WITH VEGAN CHOICES

★★ / $

30. Caracas Arepa Bar

91 East 7th Street (at First Avenue)
New York, NY 10009
212.228.5062; www.caracasarepabar.com

VENEZUELAN

Hours:	Tue-Thu 11:00 a.m. to 11:00 p.m.
	Fri-Sat 11:00 a.m. to midnight
	Sun 10:30 a.m. to 9:00 p.m.
	Closed Mon
Payment:	Cash only
Alcohol:	No
Atmosphere:	Casual dining

About the size of a large walk-in closet, Caracas Arepa
Bar is cozy and quaint and, as the menu says, vegetarian

friendly. Arepas are what you might describe as Venezuelan street food—small corn-flour-based pockets filled with melted butter or cheese and perfect for eating on the go. There are plenty of variations on the theme such as the delectable La Platanera, with cheese and sweet plantains. Though it's not a strictly vegetarian restaurant, one of the best items on the menu happens to be the Vegans Deluxe, filled with portobello mushrooms and sautéed tofu. Even with a dozen meat-free choices, the staff takes special requests and will stuff an arepa with up to two fillings of your choice. Other savory and sweet treats are available as well. At $4.50 or less per arepa, order a bunch and you can't go wrong.

FULL MENU WITH VEGETARIAN AND VEGAN CHOICES

★★★ / $$$

31. Caravan of Dreams

405 East 6th Street
(between First Avenue and Avenue A)
New York, NY 10014
212.254.1613; www.caravanofdreams.net

MULTIETHNIC

Hours:	Sun-Fri 11:00 a.m. to 11:00 p.m.
	Sat 11:00 a.m. to midnight
Payment:	Credit cards
Alcohol:	Wine and beer
Atmosphere:	Casual, comfortable dining

Don't make any assumptions based on the location, just east of 6th Street's overbearing Indian restaurant strip. Caravan of Dreams is an oasis with hanging plants, old hardwood floors, exposed brick walls, church pew banquettes, flowers on the tables, and live music nightly. If you're looking for a nice cozy place to enjoy with friends, this is it. Just arrive early because it fills up fast. Though pricey for the neighborhood, the menu is delightful. Don't order conservatively—you can get a decent burrito or stir-fry anywhere. The raw "live" flaxseed-based bruschetta appetizer is like nothing you've tried before. Angel's Caravan Feast also defies description; there's grilled polenta, mushroom gravy, grilled tempeh, tahini, and vegetables, and it all comes together perfectly. Just be sure to save some room for the vegan desserts. Main dishes from $9 to $15.

KOSHER VEGAN

★★★ / $

32. Chelsea Thai

75 Ninth Avenue
(between West 15th and West 16th Streets)
Chelsea Market Building, New York, NY 10011
212.924.2999

THAI

Hours:	Mon-Fri 10:00 a.m. to 9:45 p.m.
	Sat 11:00 a.m. to 6:45 p.m.
	Sun 11:00 a.m. to 6:00 p.m.
Payment:	Cash only
Alcohol:	No
Atmosphere:	Counter service with casual seating

Although it's located within the industrial-chic Chelsea
Market, nobody goes to Chelsea Thai for the atmosphere.
There are a few metal tables, unfinished ceilings with
exposed air ducts, and an open view of the kitchen
behind Plexiglas. If you can look beyond appearances,
you'll find that Chelsea Thai serves some of the best Thai
noodles in Manhattan. Try any of the more than two
dozen vegetarian entrées and appetizers such as Pad See
Ew, stir-fried flat noodles with fried tofu and vegetables,
or Veggie Summer Rolls served with brown plum sauce
for dipping. Everything is spicy, salty, sweet, and sour,
just like good Thai food should be. The thorough menu
lists all of the ingredients in each dish, which is great if
you have a food allergy to say, peanuts, a popular ingredient in Thai food. Tables fill up fast, so arrive early if
you want a seat. Main dishes about $7.

**FULL MENU WITH AMPLE VEGETARIAN
AND VEGAN CHOICES**

★★★ / $$

33. Chennai Garden

129 East 27th Street
(between Park and Lexington Avenues)
New York, NY 10016
212.689.1999

INDIAN

Hours:	Mon-Fri 11:30 a.m. to 3:00 p.m.,
	5:00 p.m. to 10:00 p.m.
	Sat-Sun 12:30 p.m. to 10:00 p.m.
Payment:	Credit cards
Alcohol:	No
Atmosphere:	Casual dining

It didn't take long for Chennai Garden to turn into a
"Curry Hill" favorite, even as other restaurants in the

area open and close every few months. Hidden just off the Lexington Avenue Indian-restaurant strip, it's drawing big crowds day and night. Arrive early for the bargain, weekday lunch buffet, and bring your appetite because this is Southern Indian cuisine at its best. The colorful decor makes this a great place for dining out with good friends, but it's the food that will win you over. You'll want to order extra bread to mop up every bit of the curry dishes like Palak Paneer. Chana Chat (chickpeas in a tangy sauce) is sure to impress, but the dosai and utthappam (crepe- and pancake-like dishes with spicy vegetable fillings) are the real crowd-pleasers. The coconut chutney (for dipping) may be the best in the neighborhood. Main dishes from $6 to $9.

KOSHER VEGETARIAN WITH VEGAN CHOICES

★ / $

34. Chickpea

23 Third Avenue
(between St. Mark's Place and East 9th Street)
New York, NY 10003
212.254.9500; www.chickpearestaurant.com

MIDDLE EASTERN

Hours:	Mon-Wed 10:00 a.m. to 1:00 a.m.
	Thu-Fri 10:00 a.m. to 4:00 a.m.
	Sat 10:00 a.m. to 5:00 a.m.
	Sun 10:00 a.m. to 1:00 a.m.
Payment:	Cash
Alcohol:	No
Atmosphere:	Take-out service with limited seating

If you've been looking for ordinary and overrated falafel served in a busy setting, this is the place for you. The throngs of customers might all be drunk (note the very late hours), because any sane person would be scared away by the party-minded crowds. The only redeeming thing about Chickpea is the bread, baked fresh and puffy in the way most Israeli-owned restaurants do, but it's all downhill from there. Soups taste like they came from a can. The falafel sandwich is mushy, overstuffed, and bland, though you can flavor it yourself from the unmarked bottles at the tables. The Chickplant sandwich is a good idea gone wrong, unless you like burnt eggplant. If it wasn't for the nearby NYU dormitories and students looking for a quick, cheap meal, it would be hard to imagine how this place could stay in business. Sandwiches and entrees from $3.50 to $14.

**FULL MENU WITH VEGETARIAN
AND VEGAN CHOICES**

★★★ / $$

35. Cho Dang Gol

> 55 West 35th Street
> (between Fifth and Sixth Avenues)
> New York, NY 10001
> 212.695.8222

KOREAN

Hours:	Daily 11:30 a.m. to 10:30 p.m.
Payment:	Credit cards
Alcohol:	Wine and beer
Atmosphere:	Casual dining

Don't get too excited about the sign that says "BBQ and Tofu Restaurant" because at Cho Dang Gol, like most Korean restaurants, pork has a way of showing up where it doesn't belong. The good news is that the vegetarian offerings are impressive, and select dishes can be prepared without meat upon special request. You can expect big crowds for lunch, and a considerable amount of noise for an otherwise quaint and traditionally styled restaurant, so bring along some friends and sample a variety of dishes like the Buh Sut Do Boo Bin Dae Duck (mushroom pancakes with potato and tofu). Tofu casseroles such as Ya Chae Cham Doo Boo are their specialty, served so hot that they're literally boiling at your table. If it's not spicy enough for you, then sample the assorted complimentary kimchees. Main dishes from $8 to $15.

**FULL MENU WITH VEGETARIAN
AND VEGAN CHOICES**

★★★ / $$

36. City Bakery

> 3 West 18th Street
> (between Fifth and Sixth Avenues)
> New York, NY 10011
> 212.366.1414

AMERICAN, MULTIETHNIC

Hours:	Mon-Fri 7:30 a.m. to 7:00 p.m.
	Sat 7:30 a.m. to 6:00 p.m.
	Sun 7:30 a.m. to 5:00 p.m.
Payment:	Credit cards
Alcohol:	No
Atmosphere:	Self-serve and take-out service with stylish, casual seating

As the name implies, City Bakery started out serving just desserts. Fortunately the stunning tartlets are still offered, but the menu has expanded over the years to include a tempting array of vegetarian dishes prepared with farmers' market produce at their peak of season. The cavernous decor is totally hip, with extra seating in the balcony to accommodate the big crowds at lunch hour. Menu choices change daily; you just fill up your plate or to-go container with whatever catches your eye and pay by the pound. Perfectly roasted vegetables are always available, and baked tofu is served with your choice of toppings such as Miso Dressing and Chile Sauce. Warm choices might include mini-pizzas, quesadillas, and baked macaroni and cheese on any given day. Just be sure to save room for dessert. Hot/cold buffet priced by pound, main dishes from $5 to $8.

FULL MENU WITH AMPLE VEGETARIAN AND VEGAN CHOICES

★★ / $

37. Cosmic Cantina

101 Third Avenue
(between East 12th and East 13th Streets)
New York, NY 10003
212.420.0975

MEXICAN

Hours:	Daily 11:00 a.m. to 5:00 a.m.
Payment:	Cash only
Alcohol:	Full bar
Atmosphere:	Take-out service with casual seating

Conveniently located near NYU and the New School dormitories, Cosmic Cantina stays open until the wee hours of the morning to satisfy most any hunger craving. True to what you might have come to expect from New York Tex-Mex restaurants, the food is reliably good but nothing out of the ordinary. Vegetarian options are plentiful, and almost anything on the menu can be made vegan by request at no extra cost, but the wraps are doughy and heavy. Still, the value is tough to beat. Opt for the more interesting-sounding choices such as the Roasted Veggie Burrito, packed with onion, squash, zucchini, mushrooms, peppers, cheese, and rice. Chimichangas might be the real winner if you don't mind fried food. The vibe is totally laid-back. Stop by during happy hour with some friends, order a round of margaritas, take a seat on one of the bar stools, and have a good time. Main dishes from $4 to $11.

FULL MENU WITH VEGETARIAN AND VEGAN CHOICES

★★ / $$

38. Counter

105 First Avenue
(between East 6th and East 7th Streets)
New York, NY 10003
212.982.5870

AMERICAN

Hours:	Tue-Thu & Sun 11:00 a.m. to midnight
	Fri-Sat 11:00 a.m. to 1:00 a.m.
	Mon closed
Payment:	Credit cards
Alcohol:	Wine and beer
Atmosphere:	Stylish, casual dining

The retro-hip decor may be a bigger draw than the menu at Counter. Slick Formica-topped tables, metal chairs decked out in burgundy or olive green vinyl, the slick round-bar area, and recessed overhead lighting are enough to stop a lot of people in their tracks when strolling down First Avenue. Still new-ish and trying to find itself, Counter's menu has a few gems. The Codfish Cake Platter might not resemble seafood in any form, but that doesn't mean you won't enjoy it, though the zesty coleslaw, tasty fries, and Fiestaware plates steal the show. Sandwiches vary in their appeal. If you're tired of mushy veggie burgers, stick with the satisfying Southern BBQ Po' Boy, made with smoked tofu seitan and grilled red peppers. Counter calls itself a wine bar, so the nightly organic wine-tasting specials are worth checking out. Main dishes from $9 to $14.

VEGAN

★★ / $$

39. Curly's Vegetarian Lunch

328 East 14th Street
(between First and Second Avenues)
New York, NY 10003
212.598.9998

MULTIETHNIC

Hours:	11:00 a.m. to 11:00 p.m.
Payment:	Cash
Alcohol:	Beer and sangria
Atmosphere:	Casual dining

From the same people who owned the former Veg-City Diner comes Curly's Vegetarian Lunch, located on a busy, but convenient (for East Village residents) strip of East 14th. Arguably, it can't compare with Veg-City, but depending on your tastes, it may in fact be a winner. The staff is always charming and the owner can often be found chatting it up with customers. You may find the tiny, colorful space to be quite a delight, as Curly's loyal fans clearly do. But it all comes down to the food, and a few choices here sound better than they taste. You're advised to skip the meatloaf altogether, and even favorites like the Faux Philly Cheesesteak are a bit of an acquired taste. The Cubano Nuevo sandwich is your best bet if you're looking for something flavorful and original. Curly's is destined to become a neighborhood favorite, but may not be worth going out of your way to try. Sandwiches and Entrees from $6 to $11.

VEGETARIAN WITH VEGAN CHOICES

★★★ / $$

40. Curry Leaf

99 Lexington Avenue (at East 27th Street)
New York, NY 10016
212.725.5558; www.curryleafnyc.com

INDIAN

Hours:	Daily 11:30 a.m. to 3:00 p.m.,
	5:00 p.m. to 11:00 p.m.
Payment:	Credit cards
Alcohol:	Beer and wine
Atmosphere:	Casual dining

Brought to you by the owners of herb-and-spice emporium Kalustyan's, Curry Leaf is literally surrounded by strictly vegetarian restaurants, so if the food wasn't so good here, it would seem odd to include it in this book at all. Reminiscent of East 6th Street Indian restaurants, Christmas lights line the walls. Fortunately it's subtle, and the dining room is friendly and comfortable. Just don't be surprised if the restaurant is filled to capacity during peak dinner hours; Curry Leaf's high-quality food is no secret among New Yorkers. Unlike its neighbors, you won't find any dosas here. Papa dums (lentil crackers) are complimentary, and you can't really go wrong with any of the vegetable entrées. Aloo Gobi (cauliflower and potatoes) and Malai Kofta (vegetable fritters in a creamy tomato sauce) are so tasty, you'll want to order plenty of naan bread to mop up every drop. Main dishes from $8 to $9.

**FULL MENU WITH VEGETARIAN
AND VEGAN CHOICES**

★★★ / $

41. Dil-e-punjab Deli

164 Ninth Avenue (at West 20th Street)
New York, NY 10011
212.647.9428

INDIAN

Hours:	Open 24 hours
Payment:	Cash only
Alcohol:	No
Atmosphere:	Take-out deli with limited seating

Have you ever seen a line of cabs outside a divey Indian take-out joint and wondered what the food was like? Though intriguing, most of them are Halal restaurants with limited meatless choices, with the exception of Dil-e-punjab of course. Drivers can stop by at any hour, day or night, for a quick meal of, besides the chicken kebabs, strictly vegetarian fare. If the thought of dining alongside cabbies doesn't scare you off, the decor at Dil-e-punjab certainly will, and it would be a shame because the food is really quite good. Whether or not you live or work in Chelsea, it's worth checking out. Order a bargain-priced to-go container with a few assorted curries and dal over rice, and prepare to be pleasantly surprised. Both the pureed spinach and the peas with paneer cheese are rich and flavorful, as good as you can get anywhere on Lexington Avenue or the East Village. Combo plate $5.

**ALMOST COMPLETELY VEGETARIAN
WITH VEGAN CHOICES**

★★ / $$

42. Dim Sum Go Go

5 East Broadway (near the Bowery)
New York, NY 10002
212.732.0797

CHINESE

Hours:	Daily 10:00 a.m. to 11:00 p.m.
Payment:	Credit cards
Alcohol:	No
Atmosphere:	Stylish, casual dining

If you've been put off by the dives of Chinatown, you might want to stop by Dim Sum Go Go. As luck would have it, the most stylish restaurant in the neighborhood is most definitely veggie friendly. If you can take your eyes off the boldly designed red-and-white decor for a moment, you'll notice that there are ten different varieties of meatless dumplings on the menu. For the best experience, order the sampler plate—one of each. It's a little pricey, but you'll be amazed by the colors and shapes. This is dim sum as an art. If you're in the mood for something a little more substantial, plenty of unconventional vegetarian entrées are offered as well. Mock Shark's Fin is a huge mound of egg, bean sprouts, and rice noodles—this dish may seem pricey (by Chinatown standards), but it's big enough to feed two people. Main dishes from $10 to $15.

FULL MENU WITH VEGETARIAN
AND VEGAN CHOICES

★★ / $$$
43. Diwan

148 East 48th Street
(between Third and Lexington Avenues)
New York, NY 10017
212.593.5425

INDIAN

Hours:	Mon-Thu 11:30 a.m. to 2:30 p.m.,
	5:00 p.m. to 10:30 p.m.
	Fri 11:30 a.m. to 2:30 p.m.,
	5:00 p.m. to 11:00 p.m.
	Sat 11:30 a.m. to 3:00 p.m.,
	5:00 p.m. to 11:00 p.m.
	Sun 11:30 a.m. to 3:00 p.m.,
	5:00 p.m. to 10:30 p.m.
Payment:	Credit cards
Alcohol:	Full bar
Atmosphere:	Mid- to upscale dining

Entertaining vegetarian clients in midtown is no easy task. Of course most any restaurant offers a meatless dish or two, but for a wide selection of reliable vegetarian food, Diwan may be just the restaurant you've been looking for. Business casual attire is appropriate, but you'd feel just as comfortable in a dressy suit. The decor is boldly styled yet professional. Plenty of à la carte vegetarian dishes are offered, but it's tough to beat the lunch buffet. For $12.95, you get a choice of several dishes, from Saag Paneer to Aloo Gobi. A salad bar, naan bread, and rice are all included, as well as a unique make-your-own chaat bar. Most downtown lunch buffets may be about half the price, but Diwan offers a convenient location and upscale atmosphere that other Indian restaurants can't come close to. Just don't forget to bring your corporate credit card. Main dishes from $10 to $15.

FULL MENU WITH VEGETARIAN
AND VEGAN CHOICES

★★ / $

44. Dojo

24–26 St. Mark's Place
(between Second and Third Avenues)
New York, NY 10012
212.674.9821

MULTIETHNIC

Hours:	Sun-Thu 11:30 a.m. to midnight
	Fri 11:30 a.m. to 1:00 a.m.
	Sat 10:00 a.m. to 1:00 a.m.
Alcohol:	Full bar
Payment:	Cash only
Atmosphere:	Casual dining

Other locations:

14 West 4th Street (at Mercer Street), New York, NY
10012, 212.505.8934

This East Village institution is a favorite both for its affordably priced meatless fare and for its people-watching from the outdoor seating along St. Mark's Place. Dojo may seem grungy at first, but it's nothing out of the ordinary for the neighborhood. One bite of a Hijiki Tofu Burger with Japanese BBQ sauce or a Soy Burger Sandwich, and you'll feel right at home. The newer West Village location is a little cheerier and friendlier, but it's usually teeming with NYU students. (Dojo isn't the place to come for a quiet, romantic dinner.) Other great meatless choices include Stir-fried Yaki-Soba Noodles, the Curry Yakemishi rice dish, and the ATC (avocado, tomato, and cheddar) sandwich. Prices are dirt cheap, portions are generous, and the service is so fast it will make your head spin, winning high marks for vegetarians who are short on time and cash. Main dishes from $4 to $8.

**FULL MENU WITH AMPLE VEGETARIAN
AND VEGAN CHOICES**

★★★ / $$

45. Dragonfly

47-49 Seventh Avenue South
(between Bleecker and Morton Streets)
New York, NY 10014
212.255.2848

PAN-ASIAN

Hours:	Mon-Thu noon to 11:30 p.m.
	Fri-Sat noon to 1:30 a.m.
	Sun noon to 11:00 p.m.
Payment:	Credit cards
Alcohol:	Full bar
Atmosphere:	Casual dining

In a touristy area of the West Village, Dragonfly is one of those restaurants you may not expect much from just based on looks. Pan-Asian menus are a dime a dozen in Manhattan these days, and at first this one seems no different. With a substantial number of unique-sounding meatless choices, it's worthy of closer inspection, and you won't be disappointed. The food is both high in quality and reasonably priced, not a common combination. Vegetarian Mango Chicken features julienned mango and "chicken" strips topped with an addictive citrus sauce. It's an out-of-the-ordinary, must-try dish. The meatless Peking Spare Ribs may not look anything like you'd expect, but the taste is tangy and bold. If you're tired of the same old veggie stir-fries available at take-out joints around town, you owe it to yourself to visit Dragonfly. Main dishes from $5 to $11.

**FULL MENU WITH VEGETARIAN
AND VEGAN CHOICES**

★★ / $$

46. Earthmatters

177 Ludlow Street
(between Houston and Stanton Streets)
New York, NY 10022
212.475.4180; www.earthmatters.com

MULTIETHNIC

Hours:	Daily 8:00 a.m. to 11:00 p.m.
Payment:	Credit cards
Alcohol:	Organic wine and beer
Atmosphere:	Health food market with counter service and casual seating

Located in the Lower East Side, next door to the meat-lover's heaven known as Kat's Deli, Earthmatters is first and foremost a terrific natural market, selling everything from soy milk and frozen vegetarian dinners to eco-smart health and beauty aids. Not to be outdone, the take-out counter offers a wide variety of vegetarian salads. For $8.75, the friendly staff will fill a container with an assortment, like the refreshingly sweet yam salad or the crunchy Waldorf salad. Don't expect lots of tofu and meat substitutes here—the salads are simply prepared and totally enjoyable. You get a lot of food for your money, but don't leave without trying a smoothie—Morning Thunder has granola mixed in for a hearty and satisfying texture. Unlike most health food markets, this one has plenty of comfortable seating. You can even order a glass of organic wine to enjoy with your food. Hot and cold buffet sold by weight.

MOSTLY VEGETARIAN AND VEGAN MENU

★★★ / $$

47. Eastanah

212 Lafayette Street
New York, NY 10012
212.625.9633; www.eastanah.com

INDONESIAN, MALAYSIAN

Hours:	*Mon-Thu 11:00 a.m. to 11:00 p.m.*
	Fri-Sat 11:00 a.m. to 11:30 p.m.
	Sun noon to 11:00 p.m.
Payment:	*Credit cards*
Alcohol:	*Full bar*
Atmosphere:	*Casual dining*

Borrowing influences from Chinese, Indian, and Thai cooking, the menu at Eastanah pleasantly defies definition. Knickknacks and artwork adorning the walls are like a crash course on Indonesian and Malaysian culture. With dark wood fence-post-like panels on the walls, the decor is all a little over the top, but you'll love it. Read the menu carefully—vegetable dishes like the Sautéed Water Conolvulus contain shrimp sauce. Besides that, you're in for a treat. Roti Telur is a meatless variation on the Indian dish Roti Canai, a fun-to-eat pancake served with a soup for dipping. Tofu Istimewa is a Malaysian spin on Chinese Ma Po Tofu. Tempeh Java is the hands-down winner—strips of bean curd and tempeh are coated in a sweet-and-spicy Java sauce, and cooked until crispy. Main dishes from $7 to $8.

FULL MENU WITH VEGETARIAN
AND VEGAN CHOICES

★★★ / $

48. 18 Arhans Restaurant

227 Centre Street
(between Grand and Broome Streets)
New York, NY 10013
212.941.8986; www.18arhans.com

CHINESE

Hours:	Mon-Sat noon to 7:00 p.m.
	Sun noon to 6:00 p.m.
Payment:	Cash only
Alcohol:	No
Atmosphere:	Counter service with limited casual seating

Located away from the crowds of bustling Chinatown, 18 Arhans is a bit of an oddity. This modestly decorated restaurant doubles as a Buddhist monastery, though the back area is roped off from the restaurant. Everything on the menu is simply prepared and never fussy, but very well done. If you're not a big fan of tofu, you might want to dine elsewhere. Many of the dishes feature large chunks of tofu, steamed or fried. Vegetarian BBQ Sauce, served with steamed firm tofu, broccoli, and bell peppers, is absolutely delicious. Cold Noodles with Peanut Butter Sauce features slabs of steamed tofu, chunks of cucumber, and Japanese-style fat udon noodles. Untraditional, yes, but so satisfying. Nearly everything on the menu is $5, making this one of the best values in New York City. Whatever you do, don't forget to order an Iced Citron Juice with Honey. Main dishes from $5 to $7. Limited menu on Sunday.

VEGETARIAN WITH VEGAN CHOICES

★★ / $

49. Ess-a-Bagel

831 Third Avenue
(between East 50th and East 51st Streets)
New York, NY 10022
212.980.1010

AMERICAN, BAKERY

Hours:	Mon-Thu 6:00 a.m. to 9:00 p.m.
	Fri 6:00 a.m. to 8:00 p.m.
	Sat-Sun 6:00 a.m. to 5:00 p.m.
Payment:	Credit cards
Alcohol:	No
Atmosphere:	Counter service with casual seating

Other locations:
  359 First Avenue (at East 21st Street), New York, NY
    10010, 212.260.2252

New Yorkers know a good bagel when they taste one. So what makes this bagel shop so different that it's the only one included in this book? How do eight different kinds of tofu cream cheese sound to all you vegans? Sure they've got a dozen or so varieties of regular cream cheese, but the tofu flavors are so tasty, you'll never miss the dairy. Herb, scallion, sun-dried tomato, and even walnut-raisin are just a few of the varieties. There's an eggplant salad as well, in addition to standards like egg salad. As if all that's not enticing enough, it just happens that the bagels at Ess-a are as good as they get: a little chewy, with a hearty crust on the outside and a soft texture on the inside. If you like wimpy bagels, this isn't the place for you. Sure the lines are always long, but that means turnover is high, and you're likely to get a bagel still hot from the oven during the morning rush. Bagels $2 to $3.

FULL MENU WITH VEGETARIAN AND VEGAN CHOICES

★★ / $

50. Eva's

11 West 8th Street
(between Fifth and Sixth Avenues)
New York, NY 10011
212.677.3496; www.evasvitamin.com

AMERICAN, MULTIETHNIC

Hours:	*Mon-Sat 11:00 a.m. to 11:00 p.m.*
	Sun 11:00 a.m. to 10:00 p.m.
Payment:	*Cash only*
Alcohol:	*No*
Atmosphere:	*Take-out service with casual seating*

Eva's may seem like an oddity for newcomers, but it's a way of life for loyal clientele. Step inside and take a look at the wall of autographed photos of professional athletes and celebrities who rave about the food. Serving up power-packed, high-protein meals, the menu is predictably meat heavy, but the number of meatless options will surprise you. Middle Eastern standards are offered, such as falafel, baba ghanoush, and hummus. All of the salads and many of the entrées are available with your choice of protein, including a nature burger option, but the favorite may be the Broccoli and Cheddar Cheese Quiche. With a vitamin and supplement store at the rear and the green-and-white checkerboard-themed decor, Eva's might not win any awards for style, but it's tough to beat for affordable and totally satisfying, home-style cooking. Main dishes from $3 to $10.

FULL MENU WITH VEGETARIAN AND VEGAN CHOICES

★★ / $

51. F&B

269 West 23rd Street
(between Seventh and Eighth Avenues)
New York, NY 10011
646.486.4441; www.gudtfood.com

AMERICAN

Hours:	Tue-Sat noon to 11:00 p.m.
	Sun-Mon noon to 10:00 p.m.
Payment:	Credit cards
Alcohol:	Beer and wine
Atmosphere:	Counter service with stylish,
	bar-stool seating

F&B looks like what you might get if you crossed a hot
dog joint with IKEA. The hip decor is well suited to
stylish Chelsea, though bar-stool seating is limited. Almost
everything on the menu is offered in a veggie version
made with a smoked tofu hot dog, all for under $4.
Choosing between a Veggie Prairie Dog with guacamole,
salsa, and cheddar cheese and a Watch Dog with chopped
tomatoes and garlic aioli isn't easy. Whatever you decide
on, be sure to order Pommes Frites or Sweet Potato
Frites as well. Dipping sauces come in a variety of flavors
such as blue cheese, sweet Thai chili, remoulade, and
curry tomato. Wash it all down with an imported beer,
and don't skip the desserts: beignets, rice pudding,
French ice cream, and sorbets. If that doesn't tempt
you, you can always stop by the Krispy Kreme two
doors away. Hotdogs from $3 to $4.

**FULL MENU WITH VEGETARIAN
AND VEGAN CHOICES**

★★★ / $$

52. Franchia

12 Park Avenue
(between East 34th and East 35th Streets)
New York, NY 10016
212.213.1001; www.franchia.com

KOREAN

Hours:	Mon-Sat 11:30 a.m. to 10:30 p.m.
	Sun noon to 10:00 p.m.
Payment:	Credit cards
Alcohol:	No
Atmosphere:	Stylish, mid-scale dining

Much like its sister restaurant, Hangawi, Franchia is an
oasis from the bustling area of Park Avenue and 34th
Street. Three separate dining levels make your dining

experience feel intimate, even when the restaurant is filled to capacity. Everything about the decor is striking, from the soaring ceilings to gorgeous Asian-inspired artwork, to the square-shaped dishware imprinted with Korean proverbs. (You can purchase a set of plates for yourself in the shop by the entrance.) Franchia is part teahouse and part restaurant, but defies definition. Korean standards like Bibimbap are offered, but the Pumpkin Noodles topped with a fragrant and tangy sauce are far more interesting. Or try the Spicy Kimchi Dumplings stuffed with Korean pickles. The complimentary green tea bread served with entrées may be the highlight of your meal. Main dishes from $9 to $17.

VEGAN

★★★ / $$

53. Galaxy Global Eatery

15 Irving Place (at East 15th Street),
New York, NY 10003
212.777.3631; www.galaxyglobaleatery.com

MULTIETHNIC

Hours:	Mon–Thu 8:00 a.m. to 2:30 a.m.
	Fri–Sat 8:00 a.m. to 3:30 a.m.
	Sun 8:00 a.m. to 1:30 a.m.
Payment:	Credit cards
Alcohol:	Full bar
Atmosphere:	Hip, casual dining

If you're tired of the same old vegetarian dishes, then you might want to try Galaxy, conveniently located just steps away from Irving Plaza. Stop in after a concert (since they're open almost all night long), and you'll find one entire side of their menu devoted to innovative meatless dishes. Galaxy's mission is to bring high-fiber and high-protein hemp-based cooking to the masses, but the friendly waitstaff is anything but preachy. Hempnut Edamame Cakes resemble nothing else—green, sesame-coated mounds served with a spicy mango "aioli." Sea Square is another treat, featuring lemon-tahini grilled tofu topped with "seaweed caviar." Whatever you order, don't forget to ask for a side of Yucca Fries with Spinach Banana Ketchup. Note that the already funky decor gets even hipper at night when the fiber-optic lighting in the ceiling becomes visible. Main dishes from $8 to $13.

**FULL MENU WITH VEGETARIAN
AND VEGAN CHOICES**

★★★ / $$

54. Gobo

401 Sixth Avenue
(between Waverly Place and West 8th Street)
New York, NY 10014
212.255.3242; www.goborestaurant.com

PAN-ASIAN

Hours:	Sun-Wed 11:30 a.m. to 11:15 p.m.
	Thu-Sat 11:30 a.m. to 11:45 p.m.
Payment:	Credit cards
Alcohol:	Wine and beer
Atmosphere:	Stylish, casual to mid-scale dining

Other locations:
  1426 Third Avenue (at 81st Street), New York, NY 10028,
  212.288.4686

Now you know where all the pretty vegetarians dine out. Maybe that's an exaggeration, but not by much. This restaurant is so striking, you're going to feel really out of place in a pair of blue jeans or shorts at dinner. Wear the new outfit you picked up at the Barney's warehouse sale and you'll fit right in. If your waiter can spare the time to actually serve your meal, you're sure to be impressed. This is Asian-inspired, boldly flavored food that makes it cool to be a vegetarian, feasting upon such dishes as Sesame Protein Nuggets in Sweet & Sour Sauce or Seitan Medallion in Sizzling Citrus Sauce. Steamed veggies on the side are just as dull as you'd expect, so cross your fingers and hope your entrée comes with an order of the fantastic sautéed kale. Health food fanatics may find the food to be too oily, so leave the calorie counters at home. Main dishes from $6 to $18.

VEGAN

★★ / $$

55. The Green Table

Chelsea Market Building,
75 Ninth Avenue
New York, NY 10011
212.741.9174; www.cleaverco.com

AMERICAN

Hours:	Mon-Sat noon to 9:00 p.m.
	Closed Sun
Payment:	Credit cards
Alcohol:	Beer and wine
Atmosphere:	Casual dining

Offering a bit of refuge from the crowds of bustling Chelsea Market, The Green Table seems out of place, almost like it belongs alongside a country road. Take a break between visits to Amy's Bread and the Manhattan Fruit Exchange to enjoy a glass of organic wine and peruse the daily-changing menu specials. Soups, salads, pizzas, quiches, and the "Farm Plate" are more often vegetarian than not and always sound great. Unfortunately, you might expect a little more for the prices. The cornbread Madeleines were the highlight of an otherwise lackluster veggie chili. Both the quiche and pizettes seemed tough on the occasion of this review, perhaps because they were made too far in advance and suffered from reheating. A safer bet is to order a frozen whole-wheat crust Mushroom Pot Pie or the organic Macaroni and Cheese to go and bake them up at home. Main dishes $7 to $10.

FULL MENU WITH VEGETARIAN
AND VEGAN CHOICES

★★★ / $
56. Grilled Cheese

> 168 Ludlow Street
> (between Houston and Stanton Streets)
> New York, NY 10022
> 212.982.6600

AMERICAN

Hours:	Mon-Sat 11:00 a.m. to midnight
	Sun 11:00 a.m. to 10:00 p.m.
Payment:	Cash only
Alcohol:	No
Atmosphere:	Counter service with limited casual seating

Welcome to "Comfort Food Central." Simplicity is the key to success at the Lower East Side's Grilled Cheese. Soups and salads are offered as well, but grilled cheese sandwiches are what they do best. Judging from the omnipresent crowds, downtown New Yorkers agree. First you choose between five types of cheese and a type of bread. Add toppings like tomato, onion, pickles, spinach, Dijon mustard, or pesto. For an extra dollar and a heartier sandwich, you can include grilled veggies. Finally, your creation is grilled to perfection. Variations are limitless. If you need some coaching, favorite combinations are offered such as the wonderful Grilled Motsy—fresh mozzarella, sun-dried tomato, baby spinach, basil pesto, and vinaigrette—highly recommended. Sandwiches from $4 to $6.

FULL MENU WITH AMPLE VEGETARIAN CHOICES

★★★★ / $$$

57. Hangawi

12 East 32nd Street
(between Fifth and Madison Avenues)
New York, NY 10016
212.213.0077; www.hangawirestaurant.com

KOREAN

Hours:	Mon-Thu noon to 3:00 p.m.,
	5:00 p.m. to 10:30 p.m.
	Fri noon to 3:00 p.m.,
	5:00 p.m. to 11:00 p.m.
	Sat 1:00 p.m. to 11:00 p.m.
	Sun 1:00 p.m. to 10:00 p.m.
Payment:	Credit cards
Alcohol:	No
Atmosphere:	Mid- to upscale dining

This older sister to nearby Franchia is widely regarded as the best vegetarian restaurant in New York City. Your transcendent experience starts at the door, where you check your shoes (remember to wear good socks). You sit on flat pillows, with your feet tucked into the wells below the very low tables for those of you who prefer not to sit cross-legged. Beyond the exquisite decor, the service is impeccable, as well it should be for the prices. Your waitress politely kneels by your side to take your order and serve your food. Starting off with an order of Combination Pancakes—leek, kimchi-mushroom, and mung bean—is nice, but nothing can prepare you for how good the entrées are. Crispy Mushrooms in Sweet and Sour Sauce is leaps and bounds better than similar-sounding dishes served elsewhere. Grilled Tofu Delight is bean curd at its very best. Main dishes from $15 to $20.

VEGAN

★★★ / $$

58. Haveli

100 Second Avenue (at East 6th Street)
New York, NY 10003
212.982.0533

INDIAN

Hours:	Daily noon to midnight
Payment:	Credit cards
Alcohol:	Beer and wine
Atmosphere:	Stylish, casual- to mid-scale dining

Just around the corner from the overbearing Indian strip on East 6th Street is one of the most stylish restaurants in the East Village. You can't tell much about it from the outside—the crackled windowpanes prevent you from peeking in. It's a dramatic multilevel space with contemporary lighting, hanging tapestries, and dark moody colors, perfect for intimate dinner conversation. Start off with the sweet and spicy Chana Chat appetizer, one of the best in the city. Curry dishes vary in quality and are all on the mild side. Shaag Ponir, fried cheese with fresh spinach, may be bland, but the Malai Kofta, vegetable balls in a thick tomato sauce, is a winner. Many of the curries are a bit chunky, a distinction that makes Haveli unique and worth a try, but you may want to stay clear if you've come to love the mushy, pureed curries served at most restaurants in the area. Main dishes from $8 to $10.

FULL MENU WITH VEGETARIAN

AND VEGAN CHOICES

★ / $

59. The Health Food Cafe & Luncheonette (Village Yogurt)

547 Sixth Avenue
(between West 14th and West 15th Streets)
New York, NY 10011
212.929.3752

MULTIETHNIC

Hours:	*Mon-Fri 10:30 a.m. to 8:00 p.m.*
	Sat 11:00 a.m. to 6:00 p.m.
Payment:	*Cash only*
Alcohol:	*No*
Atmosphere:	*Counter service with casual seating*

It may look like every other generic sandwich shop/deli in the city, but The Health Food Cafe & Luncheonette offers up a surprising number of meatless dishes at dirt-cheap prices. As nearby New School and Parson's students probably well know, the serving sizes are enormous. Health fanatics might fare well here, but if good taste is what you're after, you're going to be disappointed. Entrées like the Combination Fantasy, their "most popular dish," include brown rice, steamed vegetables and tofu, and veggie dumplings. Tahini dressing is served on the side, but you're going to need a lot of it to flavor this dish. The dumplings are the highlight, so you're better off ordering a plate of them with a garden salad. Sandwiches are a safer bet but still a bit dull. Better yet, order a frozen Banana Flip yogurt shake to go. Main dishes from $5 to $7.

FULL MENU WITH VEGETARIAN

AND VEGAN CHOICES

★★ / $

60. Health & Harmony

470 Hudson Street
(between Barrow and Grove Streets)
New York, NY 10014
212.691.3036

MULTIETHNIC

Hours:	Mon-Fri 9:00 a.m. to 8:30 p.m.
	Sat 10:00 a.m. to 7:30 p.m.
	Sun noon to 7:00 p.m.
Payment:	Credit cards
Alcohol:	No
Atmosphere:	Health food market, takeout only with no seating

Venture to the back of this well-stocked health food market to find the relatively hidden prepared foods counter. Besides the tuna salad, menu choices are entirely vegetarian, with lots of vegan options as well, and unlike many NYC markets, everything is prepared fresh on the premises. The zesty meatless meatballs are one of the highlights. Cold and warm salads are hearty and satisfying. The meat-free chicken salad is enjoyable as well, so it's a shame that, as is the case at most health food stores, sandwiches prepared hours in advance don't hold up very well. Besides the convenient Greenwich Village location, one of the best things about this market is the friendly staff. If you have any trouble finding what you're looking for, you can be sure that someone will come along soon to offer you some help soon. Hot and cold foods sold by weight.

MOSTLY VEGETARIAN AND VEGAN CHOICES

★★ / $

61. Healthy Chelsea

248 West 23rd Street
(between Seventh and Eighth Avenues)
New York, NY 10011
212.691.0286

AMERICAN

Hours:	Mon-Sat 10:00 a.m. to 10:00 p.m.
	Sun noon to 8:00 p.m.
Payment:	Credit cards
Alcohol:	No
Atmosphere:	Take-out service with casual bar-stool seating

Healthy Chelsea's owners couldn't have been too happy about the opening of Manhattan's first Whole Foods around the corner on Seventh Avenue, but this compact health food market has managed to survive. Maybe it has something to do with the tasty prepared food. The selection may be small, but you can eat well for not a lot of money. Besides the sandwiches, which sit wrapped for countless hours, it's tough to go wrong with whatever you order. Try ordering a cup of warm veggie chili or, even better, the rich and meatlike seitan stew with mushrooms. The zesty three-bean salad is another good choice. Unlike just about every other health food store in town, seating is available, as long as you don't mind sitting on a bar stool. Main dishes $3 to $6.

VEGETARIAN WITH VEGAN CHOICES

★★ / $$$
62. Heirloom

> 191 Orchard Street
> (between Houston and Stanton Streets)
> New York, NY 10002
> 212.228.9998

MULTIETHNIC

Hours:	5:30 p.m. to 11:00 p.m.
Payment:	Credit cards
Alcohol:	Full bar
Atmosphere:	Stylish, casual dining

A disclaimer is required because the occasion of this review was just a few days after Heirloom opened. By the time you read this, it will have been open for months, and things may have changed. In any case, the slick decor makes Heirloom a great spot for an intimate date or an outing with stylish friends—not a surprise considering the trendy Lower East Side location. Matthew Kenny, who opened the stellar and strictly raw Pure Food and Wine, is behind this newcomer, but something isn't quite right about the food. After the complimentary hush puppies are served, sadly, it's all downhill. You're paying top dollar for some of the most pretentious and absurd food NYC veggies have ever seen. It's not worth focusing too much on the menu, because it will most likely be revamped. As for right now, the textures are off-putting and some (pricey) entrees offer little or nothing for adventurous eaters. Entrees $15 to $19.

VEGETARIAN WITH VEGAN CHOICES

★★ / $

63. Hoosmoos Asli

100 Kenmare Street
(at Centre Market Place, near Lafayette Street)
New York, NY 10012
212.966.0022

ISRAELI, MIDDLE EASTERN

Hours:	Daily 10:00 a.m. to midnight
Payment:	Cash only
Alcohol:	No
Atmosphere:	Casual dining

In a city filled with run-of-the-mill Middle Eastern dives, Hoosmoos Asli stands out from the pack. First off, they actually offer table service. It may be jam-packed for lunch with just one waitress on staff, but at least you can sit down and enjoy your food in clean and comfortable quarters. Ordering the signature Hoosmoos Asli, mashed Israeli spiced chickpeas, should be a requirement. Try it with fava beans or stewed mushrooms if you're feeling adventurous, and plan on adding hot sauce, lemon juice, and salt to suit your personal taste. The real standout is the accompanying pita bread. Forget about the chewy, lifeless pocket breads you've come to know well at other falafel joints—the Israeli-style pita here is fresh, soft, and fluffy. On bread like this, an otherwise ordinary falafel sandwich is elevated to new heights. Main dishes from $4 to $8.

**FULL KOSHER MENU WITH VEGETARIAN
AND VEGAN CHOICES**

★★ / $$

64. House of Vegetarian

68 Mott Street (between Bayard and Canal Streets)
New York, NY 10013
212.226.6572

CHINESE

Hours:	Daily 11:00 a.m. to 10:30 p.m.
Payment:	Cash only
Alcohol:	No
Atmosphere:	Casual dining

Like its sister restaurant Vegetarian Dim Sum House on Pell Street, House of Vegetarian isn't much to look at, but it's cleaner and more comfortable than most of the restaurants in the neighborhood. Skip the dumplings altogether, and stick with the more reliable entrées.

The tasty Fried Noodles in Gravy with Sautéed Tofu is available in two sizes, but even the smaller one is generously portioned. Will it turn you into a tofu lover? Probably not. General Tso's Chicken is richly flavored; the fried bean curd is crispy on the outside and softer inside, and not fussy at all. "Not fussy" pretty well sums up House of Vegetarian; the reasonably priced food is consistently good, much the way you'd expect from Chinatown, but nothing here is fancy or stylish like the trendier veggie Pan-Asian restaurants in Greenwich Village. Main dishes from $8 to $12.

VEGAN

★★★ / $

65. Hummus Place

99 MacDougal Street
(between West 3rd and Bleecker Streets)
New York, NY 10012
212.533.3089

MIDDLE EASTERN

Hours:	Sun-Thu 11:00 a.m. to midnight
	Fri-Sat 11:00 a.m. to 2:00 a.m.
Payment:	Cash
Alcohol:	No
Atmosphere:	Casual dining

Other Locations:
  109 St. Mark's Place (between First Avenue and Avenue A),
  212.529.9198

With two convenient locations and counting, keep your fingers crossed that Hummus Place opens near you. The menu is so short, you'll be able to recite it by heart after just one visit. Basically, you decide if you want hummus foul (chickpeas and fava beans), masabacha (chickpeas and tahini) or just with tahini. You really can't go wrong. Hummus is made fresh throughout the day, and the puffy Israeli-style pita breads (white or wheat) are so much better than the stale, flat variety you may be used to. Hummus Place keeps late hours, like most restaurants in the MacDougal-Bleecker Street area, and though it can fill up to capacity in a matter of moments, don't let anything keep you away. This is real, pure, satisfying food at its best. Other places in town may have a similar menu, but this is the real thing and the value is unbeatable. Entrees from $4 to $5.

VEGETARIAN WITH VEGAN CHOICES

★★ / $

66. India Fast Food

SE Corner of East 53rd Street and Park Avenue,
New York, NY

INDIAN

Hours:	Mon-Fri 11:00 a.m. to 4:00 p.m.
Payment:	Cash only
Alcohol:	No
Atmosphere:	Take-out cart service only

If the barometer of success for take-out lunch carts is
the length of the line, then India Fast Food must be a
winner. For vegetarian midtown office workers who have
grown tired of over-priced delis serving low-grade wraps
and salads, it's definitely a welcome change of pace. The
crowd never dwindles, but as the name implies, the line
moves quickly. Besides the option of samosas, your
choice is simple: would you like a vegetarian or nonvege-
tarian combination platter? For a bargain price you get
three curries, rice, naan bread, and a little green salad.
Curry choices such as Malai Kofta and Green Squash Aloo
change daily, so eating here is a bit of a surprise. While
maybe not the best in town, the food is reliably good for
a lunch cart, not to mention a little spicy. If you ever get
tired of the food at Govinda's just a block away on busy
Park Avenue, give India Fast Food a try. Combo plate $6.

**FULL MENU WITH VEGETARIAN
AND VEGAN CHOICES**

★★★ / $

67. Indian Bread Co.

194 Bleecker Street
(between Sixth Avenue and MacDougal Street)
New York, NY 10012
212.228.1909; www.indianbreadco.com

INDIAN

Hours:	Sun noon to 10:00 p.m.
	Mon-Thu noon to 11:00 p.m.
	Fri-Sat noon to 1:00 a.m.
Payment:	Credit cards
Alcohol:	No
Atmosphere:	Take-out service with limited seating

Indian fast food joints like this are popping up around
the city, serving a cross between authentic Indian street
food and the ho-hum wraps and paninis sold at hundreds
of lunch-spot delis around town. Indian Bread Co. is one
of the first of its kind and is likely to remain one of the

best. Carnivores and vegetarians will both feel right at home with the full menu, but the meatless options are all winners, especially if you like your food with a bit of a "kick." And the variety of sandwich styles will keep you coming back for more. The naaninis are made from a grilled naan flatbread with fillings like saag paneer (spinach) or marinated vegetables. The slightly messy naanwiches are more like a pocket sandwich, the kathi rolls are convenient wraps, one served with egg and caramelized onions, and don't miss the potato-stuffed paratha sandwiches. Sandwiches from $3.50 to $7.

FULL MENU WITH VEGETARIAN
AND VEGAN CHOICES

★★ / $
68. Integral Yoga Natural Foods

229 West 13th Street
(between Seventh and Eighth Avenues)
New York, NY 10013
212.243.2642; www.iynaturalfoods.com

MULTIETHNIC

Hours:	Mon-Fri 9:00 a.m. to 9:30 p.m.
	Sat-Sun 9:00 a.m. to 8:30 p.m.
Payment:	Credit cards
Alcohol:	No
Atmosphere:	Market with take-out counter and no seating

With a yoga center, food market, and vitamin shop, Integral Yoga seems to be taking over this block of West 13th Street. That's good news because, as health food markets go, this one is a winner. Relatively hidden at the back you'll find the prepared food including a hot buffet table, veggie burgers, fresh juices, sandwiches, soups, and more. It's tough to get a view of what you're ordering, due to the crowded aisles and poor lighting, but don't let that scare you away. Unlike LifeThyme and Health & Harmony, this market is strictly vegetarian (vegan actually), and the food is a step up in taste and quality. Arrive early for the best selection, fill up a platter with the likes of veggie duck with bok choy, stuffed bean curd, and curried potato and squash, and enjoy. The veggie sushi is tasty, but like any premade sushi, the seaweed wrappers can be chewy. Hot buffet sold by weight.

VEGAN

★★★ / $$

69. Itzocan Café

438 East 9th Street
(between First Avenue and Avenue A)
New York, NY 10009
212.677.5856

MEXICAN

Hours:	Daily 11:00 a.m. to midnight
Payment:	Cash only
Alcohol:	No
Atmosphere:	Casual dining

Forget what you know about affordably priced Mexican food in New York City—Itzocan serves anything but standard fare. Sure they offer burritos and quesadillas, but calling this Tex-Mex food would be a disservice. The lunch menu is very veggie friendly, not to mention a great value for such high quality. Quesadillas just don't get any better than one filled with mushrooms, huitlacoche, poblano peppers, and cheese. If you're really feeling adventurous, you might opt for the Cactus Leaf Burrito, made with pickled jalapeños, tomatoes, and cilantro. Though small, Itzocan's decor features just enough decorative touches, including the sculpted relief walls and Oaxacan knick-knacks, to make this a charming place for dining in. To get started, order a side of guacamole with homemade tortilla chips and a couple of fruity Mexican sodas, and you really can't go wrong. Main dishes from $6 to $10.

**FULL MENU WITH VEGETARIAN
AND VEGAN CHOICES**

★★★ / $$

70. Jaiya Thai

396 Third Avenue
(between East 28th and East 29th Streets)
New York, NY 10016
212.889.1330; www.jaiya.com

THAI

Hours:	Mon-Fri 11:30 a.m. to midnight
	Sat noon to midnight
	Sun 5:00 p.m. to midnight
Payment:	Credit cards
Alcohol:	Full bar
Atmosphere:	Casual dining

Other locations:

1569 Third Avenue (between East 88th and East 89th Streets), New York, NY 10128, 212.889.1330

For really well prepared food and creative meatless offerings, Jaiya is at the top of a very short list. Even if you've been to a dozen other Thai restaurants in the city, you've probably never had Thai like this before. Unlike most restaurants where the veggie dishes are an afterthought, offering tofu as a substitute for beef or chicken, Jaiya's menu is almost entirely unique. Where else can you find meatless Mee Krob, crispy rice noodles with a tangy and spicy sauce? Spicy Gluten and Mushroom Salad is served slightly warm with a chile-and-lime-based dressing that just has to be tasted. Vegetarian "duck" and "chicken" are available with any sauce on the menu, including the fragrant and zesty ginger-basil sauce, and the texture is fantastic. Curries are a favorite too. One downside: prices are high, so you might want to stop by Jaiya for a special occasion when you can splurge. Main dishes from $10 to $14.

**FULL MENU WITH VEGETARIAN
AND VEGAN CHOICES**

★★★ / $$$

71. Josie's

565 Third Avenue
(between East 37th and East 38th Streets)
New York, NY 10016
212.769.1212; www.josiesnyc.com

MULTIETHNIC

Hours:	Mon-Wed noon to 11:00 p.m.
	Thu-Fri noon to midnight
	Sat 11:30 a.m. to midnight
	Sun 11:00 a.m. to 11:00 p.m.
Payment:	Credit cards
Alcohol:	Full bar
Atmosphere:	Stylish, casual to mid-scale dining;

Other locations:

300 Amsterdam Avenue (at West 74th Street), New York, NY 10023, 212.769.1212

From plate presentation to the contemporary decor, look no further for healthy cooking with style. Josie's is just the spot for a date with someone you want to impress or for a night out with good friends. Just be sure to call ahead for a reservation because they're often filled to capacity. Enjoy the complimentary tasty carrot dip and fresh bread while you peruse the menu—everything at Josie's is dairy-free, so meatless dishes are entirely vegan. It's tough for adventurous eaters to go wrong here, from the Broccoli- and Yukon Gold Potato–stuffed Dumplings with a tomato-truffle oil coulis, to affordable sandwich entrées such as the open-faced Grilled Portobello Mushroom Sandwich. For a new twist on a classic, order Penne Pasta with

Sautéed Shiitake Mushrooms and a soy "cream" vodka sauce, or the Roasted Vegetarian "Meat" Loaf with rosemary au jus. Main dishes from $9 to $15.

FULL MENU WITH VEGAN CHOICES

★★ / $$

72. Jubb's Longevity

508 East 12th Street (between Avenues A and B)
New York, NY 10009
212.353.5000; www.jubbslongevity.com

MULTIETHNIC

Hours:	Daily 11:00 a.m. to 9:00 p.m.
Payment:	Cash only
Alcohol:	No
Atmosphere:	Take-out service only

With herbal remedies and other health products lining the wall, passersby might not even notice that Jubb's has a take-out counter. A few seats and tables for dining in would be nice, but on a pretty day you can park yourself on one of the benches outside. As with most any prepared raw vegan food, everything is served cold, whether you order a burger, a pizza, or anything else. With no menus, ordering can be a bit of a mystery. The Life Food Casserole is topped with hijiki and packed with nuts and grains, and the cabbage-wrapped "brajiole" is smothered in a thick and zesty sauce and packed with nuts and grains as well. Consult with the staff for more details than that, and try the freshly made Nut Milk while you're at it. For a real treat, order a slice of the chilly and slightly sweet Carob Cheesecake—just close your eyes, don't think about the peculiar olive green color, and enjoy. Main dishes from $6 to $10.

VEGAN

★★ / $

73. Kalustayan's

123 Lexington Avenue
(between East 28th and East 29th Streets)
New York, NY 10016
212.685.3451; www.kalustyans.com

INDIAN, MIDDLE EASTERN

Hours:	Mon-Sat 10:00 a.m. to 8:00 p.m.
	Sun 11:00 a.m. to 7:00 p.m.
Payment:	Credit cards
Alcohol:	No
Atmosphere:	Market with counter service and casual seating

It's no secret that Kalustayan's is one of the best specialty food markets in the city, offering everything from uncommon herbs and spices, to nuts, oils, chutneys, pickles, relish, sauces, and more. The upstairs vegetarian café, on the other hand, is almost entirely hidden from view. Imported cheeses like kefalotiri and paneer as well as a variety of olives are sold from behind the counter. All kinds of meatless Middle Eastern platters and sandwiches are offered, such as hummus, baba ganoujh, and stuffed grape leaves. If the lentil fritters or anything else sounds unfamiliar, don't be surprised if the friendly staff hands you a taste sample to help you make up your mind. Affordable prices and ample portions make up for the limited seating. Just take your order to go and check the refrigerator cases downstairs for fantastic ready-to-serve Indian dips and sauces, perfect with pita bread. Sandwiches from $3 to $5.

VEGETARIAN WITH VEGAN OFFERINGS

★★ / $$

74. Kate's Joint

58 Avenue B (at East 4th Street)
New York, NY 10009
212.777.7059

AMERICAN

Hours:	Sun-Thu 9:00 a.m. to midnight
	Fri-Sat 9:00 a.m. to 2:00 a.m.
Alcohol:	Full bar
Payment:	Credit cards
Atmosphere:	Casual dining

Just like the East Village itself, Kate's Joint is laid-back, totally unfussy, and packed with eclectic locals. It just happens to be totally vegetarian as well. Even with the kitschy lace curtains in the windows, no one comes here for the decor. The veggie vibe though is very appealing, and the "infamous" burgers are a big draw. You won't be disappointed with any of them, but it doesn't get much better than the Ranch Burger smothered in BBQ sauce, with onion rings in the burger for a bit of crunch. All of the burgers and sandwiches come with either mashed potatoes and gravy or french fries, both a good choice. The rest of the menu is a bit less reliable. Veggie hotdogs, even the Chili Dawg, are uninspiring, and some of the entrées, like the Shepherd's Pie, are heavy and dull. Stick with the burgers, and save some room for a slice of vegan cheesecake. Main dishes from $5 to $11.

VEGETARIAN WITH VEGAN CHOICES

★★★ / $$

75. Khyber Pass

> 34 St. Mark's Place
> (between Second and Third Avenues)
> New York, NY 10003
> 212.473.0989
>
> **AFGHANI**
>
> | | |
> |---|---|
> | **Hours:** | Daily noon to midnight |
> | **Payment:** | Credit cards |
> | **Alcohol:** | Beer and wine |
> | **Atmosphere:** | Casual dining |

Tapestries adorning the walls, embroidered tablecloths, and dim lighting all add to the moody ambiance at Khyber Pass, but the experience will be even better if you can score one of the window-front tables where you sit cross-legged on pillows. If you'd thought that Afghani food is a meat-friendly cuisine, you wouldn't be wrong. It's just that Afghani vegetable dishes are so exciting—you've probably never tried food like this before. The best bet is to bring some friends along and share a bunch of dishes. Boulanee Kachaloo, potato-filled turnovers with a cool yogurt dip, are a great way to start off, but nothing can prepare you for entrées like Bourance Baunjaun (melt-in-your-mouth eggplant) and Quorma Kadu (sweet and tangy pumpkin sautéed with tomato and onion). These are boldly flavored dishes, perfect for the culinarily adventurous vegetarian. Main dishes from $7 to $8.

**FULL MENU WITH VEGETARIAN
AND VEGAN CHOICES**

★★★ / $

76. Kitchen Market

> 218 Eighth Avenue (at West 21st Street)
> New York, NY 10011
> 212.243.4433; www.kitchenmarket.com
>
> **MEXICAN**
>
> | | |
> |---|---|
> | **Hours:** | Mon-Fri 9:00 a.m. to 11:00 p.m. |
> | | Sat-Sun 11:00 a.m. to 11:00 p.m. |
> | **Payment:** | Credit cards |
> | **Alcohol:** | No |
> | **Atmosphere:** | Take-out service only |

It's not easy to satisfy a burrito craving in New York City, but if you don't mind taking your order to go, Kitchen Market is up to the task. This narrow space (owned by the same people as Bright Food Shop next door) doubles as a Mexican specialty ingredient market, so don't expect much breathing room or any seating. You can, however, expect a very veggie-friendly menu with out-of-the-ordinary filling options like Green Chile Posole, Roasted Eggplant with Queso Blanco, and Cactus & Vegetable Stew. Not in the mood for a burrito? Try the New Mexico Tortilla Pie or Smoky Tomato Corn Soup. If you're not rushing to Kitchen Market just yet, here's a little more persuading: the fresh and impressively soft tortillas are made on the premises, and are available in a variety of flavors such as whole wheat, spinach, tomato, and spicy jalapeño. Burritos from $7 to $10.

FULL MENU WITH VEGETARIAN

AND VEGAN CHOICES

★★★ / $

77. Kiva Cafe

229 Hudson Street
(between Broome and Canal Streets)
New York, NY 10013
212.229.0898

AMERICAN

Hours:	*Mon-Fri 8:00 a.m. to 7:00 p.m.*
	Sun noon to 6:00 p.m.
	Closed Sat
Payment:	*Credit cards*
Alcohol:	*Wine and beer*
Atmosphere:	*Stylish, casual dining*

Keep your fingers crossed that word doesn't get out about Kiva Café. There are only a dozen or so seats, although the cute garden area helps when the weather is nice, and once you've eaten here, it's going to become your new favorite lunch spot. (Now if someone could just persuade them to move the restaurant to a more convenient location?) If you live or work anywhere near Tribeca or Soho, you owe it to yourself to stop by. Tranquil music, friendly service, and the casual but chic decor will make you feel right at home. As for the food, imagine the most delicate pastry you've ever tried, filled with mushrooms, caramelized onions, and smoked mozzarella—they call it the Spirito, but you'll call it heaven. Daily soup specials are a delight, not to be outdone by the warm Tre Formaggi sandwich served on olive bread so good, you'll be asking if they sell it by the loaf. Sandwiches and tarts from $5 to $7.

FULL MENU WITH VEGETARIAN

AND VEGAN CHOICES

★★ / $

78. Kwik Meal

SW Corner of West 45th Street and Sixth Avenue,
New York, NY

MIDDLE EASTERN

Hours:	Daily 11:00 a.m. to 8:00 p.m.
Payment:	Cash only
Alcohol:	No
Atmosphere:	Take-out cart service only

Other locations:

Vanderbuilt Avenue at East 46th Street;
Fifth Avenue at West 45th Street

Can a former Russian Tea Room chef find satisfaction
running a midtown lunch cart? Apparently the answer is
yes. Chef M. D. Rahman serves up a full menu of kabobs
and even pastrami on this busy corner, staying late
enough for dinner-hour diners, but you need only con-
cern yourself with the falafel sandwich. Prepared fresh
to order, falafel balls are fried to a perfect texture, and
the laffah-style pita bread is tossed on the griddle until
it turns slightly crispy as well. (A note for hard-core
vegetarians: meat is being cooked just inches away.)
Assembly is key to Kwik Meal's success. With the hot laf-
fah bread laid flat, falafel and toppings like pickles and a
cabbage-based "slaw" are piled on, and the entire thing is
wrapped closed, much like a soft taco. It's definitely
worth a try, and if you work in midtown, you may find
yourself coming back often. Sandwiches from $4 to $6.

**FULL MENU WITH VEGETARIAN
AND VEGAN CHOICES**

★★ / $$

79. Lemongrass Grill

74-76 Seventh Avenue South
(at Barrow Street near Bleecker Street)
New York, NY 10014
212.242.0606

THAI

Hours:	Daily noon to 11:00 p.m.
Payment:	Credit
Alcohol:	Beer and wine
Atmosphere:	Casual dining

Other locations:

2534 Broadway (between West 94th and West 95th
Streets), New York, NY 10025, 212.666.0888;

138 East 34th Street (between Lexington and Third
   Avenues), New York, NY 10016, 212.213.3317;
80 University Place (at East 11th Street), New York, NY
   10003, 212.604.9870;
53 Avenue A (at East 4th Street), New York, NY 10009,
   212.674.3538;
61A Seventh Avenue (between Berkeley and Lincoln Places),
   Park Slope, Brooklyn, NY 11217, 718.399.7100

Much as Baluchi's has done for Indian food, Lemongrass
Grill attempts to bring Thai food to the masses with
reasonable prices and upbeat atmosphere in popular
neighborhoods like the East and West Villages. The fact
that those neighborhoods are already packed with Thai
restaurants doesn't seem to matter a bit, and for a
growing chain with six locations, the food is better
than you'd expect. Judged by the speedy and friendly
waitservice alone, Lemongrass is a winner. Where they
go wrong is with respect to onions and peppers, also
known as "filler" in Thai cooking. Portions look massive,
but you're left with a pile of onions on your plate
when you're finished. Still, you won't be disappointed
if you stop by to try the appealing Cashew Tofu and
the very rich and peanuty Massaman Curry. Main dishes
from $7 to $9.

**FULL MENU WITH VEGETARIAN
AND VEGAN CHOICES**

★★★ / $$

8o. Life Cafe

343 East 10th Street (at Avenue B)
New York, NY 10009
212.477.8791; www.lifecafenyc.com

AMERICAN, MULTIETHNIC

Hours:	Sun–Thu 10:00 a.m. to midnight
	Fri–Sat 10:00 a.m. to 2:00 a.m.
Payment:	Credit cards
Alcohol:	Full bar
Atmosphere:	Casual dining

Other locations:

983 Flushing Avenue, Bushwick, Brooklyn, NY 10026,
   718.386.1133

Located on the corner of Tompkins Square Park in the
East Village, Life Cafe offers up a surprising number of
vegan dishes for a restaurant with a full menu. Skip
over the veggie burgers and salads and feast your eyes
and taste buds on offerings like the Vegan Quesadilla,
Vegan Nachos, and the particularly good Seitan Philly

Steak sandwich. Be sure to include the optional smoky tempeh bacon with the Grilled Soy Cheese, Avocado, and Tomato Sandwich (possibly the best vegan sandwich in New York City). The decor is typical of the neighborhood: tin ceilings, tiled floors, and a bit grungy but hip, brought to life with old, decoupaged Life magazine photos on the tabletops (hence the name). The outdoor seating is great for people-watching or running into friends. While maybe not as affordable as other restaurants in the area, you can't beat the friendly atmosphere. Main dishes from $8 to $13.

FULL MENU WITH VEGAN OPTIONS

★★ / $

81. LifeThyme Market

410 Sixth Avenue
(between West 8th and West 9th Streets)
New York, NY 10011
212.420.9099

MULTIETHNIC

Hours:	Mon-Fri 8:00 a.m. to 10:00 p.m.
	Sat-Sun 9:00 a.m. to 10:00 p.m.
Payment:	Credit cards
Alcohol:	No
Atmosphere:	Health food market, takeout with no seating

Other locations:
  2275 Broadway (at West 82nd Street), New York, NY
  10024, 212.721.9000

LifeThyme makes up for cramped quarters with an amazing array of vegetarian and health food products, from vitamins to frozen vegetarian dinners to whole grains and beans. What makes this market different from so many others in the neighborhood is its extensive selection of prepared foods. Hot and cold buffet tables are almost exclusively vegetarian, offering Curried Rice Salad, Vegetarian Chili, Organic Baked Tofu, and more. Just fill up a to-go container and pay by the pound at the register. Refrigerator cases at the back offer vegetarian entrées in generous portion sizes, including Vegan Samosas and raw "pizzas," and the friendly staff is happy to help you make a selection. Vegan desserts, like all of the food, are made right on the premises, unlike most other health food markets. A word of warning: even desserts like the Chocolate Mint Mousse Tart taste healthy. Hot and cold buffet sold by weight.

**KOSHER MENU WITH VEGETARIAN
AND VEGAN CHOICES**

★★★ / $

82. Liquiteria at Lucky's

170 Second Avenue (at East 11th Street)
New York, NY 10003
212.358.0300

JUICE BAR

Hours:	*Mon-Fri 7:30 a.m. to 9:30 p.m.*
	Sat-Sun 9:00 a.m. to 10:00 p.m.
Payment:	*Cash only*
Alcohol:	*No*
Atmosphere:	*Take-out service with limited bar-stool seating*

These days freshly blended juices and smoothies are easy to come by in the Big Apple, but owner Doug Green is nearly a legend in vegetarian circles. Since the original Lucky's on Houston Street closed down, Doug's Liquiteria at Lucky's has taken over as king of the juice joints. Even for those who aren't in the know, everything about this place is inviting, from the hip vibe and great East Village location to the friendly staff. Don't be surprised if you're offered a free sample of the smoothie of the day every time you visit. You'll find something on the "Liquid Pharmacy" menu to cure what ails you: Energy Blast, Fat Burner, Mental Master. If you have to eat on the run, the "Liquid Meals" are just what they claim, like the fantastic Soy to the World, fortified with soy milk and wheat germ. Meatless burgers and sandwiches are offered as well. Juices and smoothies from $5 to $8.

VEGETARIAN WITH VEGAN CHOICES

★★★ / $$

83. Little Seoul

232 Seventh Avenue
(between West 23rd and West 24th Streets)
New York, NY 10011
917.606.1415

JAPANESE, KOREAN

Hours:	*Mon-Fri 11:00 a.m. to 11:00 p.m.*
	Sat noon to 11:00 p.m.
	Sun noon to 10:00 p.m.
Payment:	*Credit cards*
Alcohol:	*Wine and beer*
Atmosphere:	*Casual dining*

How many times has this happened to you? A bunch of nonveggie friends invite you to go out for sushi, and you get stuck eating California rolls and vegetable tempura. Here comes Togi to the rescue with sixteen vegetarian sushi options: Asparagus Rolls, Shiitake Mushroom Rolls, Tofu & Kimchi Rolls, and more. Still not satisfied? How about ten Korean entrées available in meatless versions, like Bi Bim Bap with tofu? There are appetizers as well, such as Tofu BBQ, featuring smoky grilled slabs of tofu in a delicate sauce. Meatless dishes are hidden all over the menu, and everything is prepared to perfection. This attractive restaurant has only one downside. It's just not big enough to handle the lunch hour crowds. Don't be surprised if there's a wait for a table, and try to forgive the undermanned waitstaff. The food more than makes up for any inconvenience. Sushi and main dishes from $5 to $10.

**FULL MENU WITH VEGETARIAN
AND VEGAN CHOICES**

★★★★ / $$$

84. Lupa

170 Thompson Street
(between Bleecker and Houston Streets)
New York, NY 10012
212.982.5089; www.luparestaurant.com

ITALIAN

Hours:	Daily noon to 2:30 p.m.,
	5:00 p.m. to 11:30 p.m.
Payment:	Credit cards
Alcohol:	Full bar
Atmosphere:	Stylish, mid-scale dining

Chef Mario Batali has done it again, but unlike at nearby Babbo, a meal at Lupa won't cost you an entire paycheck. Though it's far from a meatless paradise, Lupa is a favorite among vegetarians for good reason. First there's the impeccable service. Then there are the antipasti: charred leeks with egg; citrus and fennel; radicchio "farcito"; beets and ginger. Order an assortment plate and share, or try the Escarole, Walnuts, Red Onion, and Pecorino Salad. Cheese lovers will be in heaven—again, order an assortment and don't be afraid to ask the knowledgeable staff for assistance. (Also ask for help in pairing your food with an appropriate bottle of wine from the extensive but sensibly priced list.) Veggie pastas, though limited, are stunning. One word sums up the Farro Spaghettini with Spicy Cauliflower Ragu or the Linguini Fini with Meyer Lemon and Olive Oil—perfect. Main dishes from $11 to $16.

**FULL MENU WITH VEGETARIAN
AND VEGAN CHOICES**

★★★ / $$

85. Lupe's East L.A. Kitchen

110 Sixth Avenue (at Watts Street)
New York, NY 10013
212.966.1326

MEXICAN

Hours:	Sun-Tue 11:30 a.m. to 11:00 p.m.
	Wed-Sat 11:30 a.m. to midnight
Payment:	Cash only
Alcohol:	Full bar
Atmosphere:	Casual dining

At the very edge of Soho, away from the throngs of fashionistas, Lupe's delivers just what the name promises, a taste of L.A. Mexican, and dispels the myth that you can't get decent Tex-Mex food in the Big Apple. Everything about this restaurant is upbeat, yet laid-back and casual too. A pair of cool blue jeans seems to be the unwritten dress code, but the real fun starts when the food comes. Forget what you think you know about meatless Tex-Mex, i.e., rubbery tortillas, watery salsas, and lifeless fillings. Lupe's Spinach Enchilada is as good as it gets. With the exception of the tangy, dairy-free Chili Verde, vegans are out of luck because the spicy enchiladas are dripping with cheese. Most of the tasty burritos contain cheese as well, but it's hard to argue with success when you try the Super Vegetarian Burrito with your choice of red or green chili sauce. Main dishes from $7 to $8.

FULL MENU WITH VEGETARIAN CHOICES

★★ / $$

86. Madras Cafe

79 Second Avenue
(between East 4th and East 5th Streets)
New York, NY 10003
212.254.8002

INDIAN

Hours:	Mon-Sat 1:00 p.m. to 10:45 p.m.
	Sun 1:00 p.m. to 9:45 p.m.
Payment:	Credit cards
Alcohol:	Beer and wine
Atmosphere:	Casual dining

Nearby the overbearing 6th Street Indian strip, Madras Cafe is the only strictly vegetarian, southern Indian restaurant in the neighborhood. Now if they'd just give the dark and gloomy dining room a makeover, hire some better waiters, and change the music, they'd be on to something good. If you're unwilling to make the trip up to Lexington Avenue's Curry Hill for really good veggie Indian food, Madras Cafe is pretty reliable. Nothing stands out as a clear winner, but you're in for a good meal. Skip the overly crunchy Masala Vada lentil and split pea fritters, and unless you love onions, pass on the Masala Dosa as well. Order the whole wheat roti and paratha breads and some curry dishes like the slightly sweet Paneer Tikki Masala and share. Try the Kofta Curry (vegetable dumplings in a tomato-curry sauce) and the Madras Curry made with textured vegetable protein too. Main dishes from $8 to $9.

VEGETARIAN WITH VEGAN CHOICES

★★ / $$

87. Madras Mahal

104 Lexington Avenue
(between East 27th and East 28th Streets)
New York, NY 10016
212.684.4010; www.madrasmahal.com

INDIAN

Hours:	Mon-Thu 11:30 a.m. to 3:00 p.m.,
	5:00 p.m. to 10:00 p.m.
	Fri 11:30 a.m. to 3:00 p.m.,
	5:00 p.m. to 10:30 p.m.
	Sat noon to 10:30 p.m.
	Sun noon to 10:00 p.m.
Payment:	Credit cards
Alcohol:	Beer
Atmosphere:	Casual dining

With four vegetarian southern Indian restaurants located within a one-block radius, Madras Mahal is up against some tough competition. Where it loses out is with respect to the ambiance, or more appropriate, the lack of it. Over-lit and in need of a paint job, they seem to attract a lot of families with young children. Romantic Pongal next door is too quiet and cozy for that, so maybe Madras Mahal has found its niche. Still, it would be nice if the smell from the kitchen wasn't so overbearing. Perhaps the waitstaff could be a little more attentive as well. It's a shame because the curries are well prepared, including Chana Saag (chickpeas and creamed spinach) and Aloo Gobi (mildly spiced potatoes and cauliflower). Dosas are a bit ordinary—you're better off going next door to Saravana Bhavan Dosa Hut if you have a craving to satisfy. Main dishes from $6 to $9.

KOSHER VEGETARIAN WITH VEGAN CHOICES

★★★ / $

88. Mamoun's Falafel

119 Macdougal Street
New York, NY 10012
212.674.8685; www.mamounsfalafel.com

MIDDLE EASTERN

Hours:	Daily 10:00 a.m. to 5:00 a.m.
Payment:	Cash only
Alcohol:	No
Atmosphere:	Counter service only, limited seating

Other locations:

324 Main Street, Middletown, CT 06457, 860.346.4646;
85 Howe Street, New Haven, CT 06511, 203.562.8444

With a Middle Eastern take-out joint located on nearly every other block of lower Manhattan, you might wonder, "Aren't all falafel sandwiches the same?" One bite of a falafel from Mamoun's and you'll know just how silly a question that is. As almost any NYU student can tell you, Mamoun's is the king of downtown falafel. Apparently the restaurant is stuck in a time-warp, because the prices never increase. For just $2.50, you have a choice of a falafel, baba ghanoush, or hummus sandwich. You can spend more on a platter, but with almost no seating and a constant line, it's just not worth the trouble. Get your sandwich to go, and if you need to sit down, stroll over to nearby Washington Square Park. If you've just left one of the bars on Bleecker Street with a serious hunger to satisfy, stroll over to Mamoun's. It's open till the wee hours of the morning, every day of the year. Sandwiches from $3 to $5.

**FULL MENU WITH VEGETARIAN
AND VEGAN CHOICES**

★★★ / $$

89. Mana

646 Amsterdam Avenue
(between West 91st and West 92nd Avenue)
New York, NY 10025
212.787.1110

MULTIETHNIC

Hours:	Daily noon to 9:30 p.m.
Payment:	Credit cards
Alcohol:	No
Atmosphere:	Casual dining

Though it's up against a fair amount of competition in the cluttered "healthy vegetarian/fish category," Mana stands out from the crowd. As soon as you walk in off tree-lined Amsterdam Avenue, you notice the bright and friendly decor: adobe-style walls, exposed brick, and large windows facing a pretty church. Either all of the customers are regulars or the cheerful staff has a talent for making everyone feel welcome. Appetizer portions for dishes like ginger- and garlic-flavored Chinese Greens and Shiitake Mushrooms are massive, and salads are served with a terrific carrot dressing. There are plenty of Japanese items on the menu (soba, tempura, veggie sushi), with some pasta choices, an Indian curry, and even a Mexican-style dish made with tortillas, beans, and rice thrown in. Don't worry about defining Mana; just relax and enjoy yourself. Main dishes from $9 to $13.

MOSTLY VEGETARIAN AND VEGAN CHOICES WITH SEAFOOD

★★ / $$
90. Mandoo Bar

71 University Place
(between East 10th and East 11th Streets)
New York, NY 10003
212.358.0400

KOREAN

Hours:	Mon-Fri 11:30 a.m. to 11:00 p.m.
	Sat-Sun 11:00 a.m. to midnight
Payment:	Credit cards
Alcohol:	Beer and wine
Atmosphere:	Casual dining

Other Locations:

2 West 32nd Street (between Fifth Avenue and Broadway), New York, NY 10001, 212.279.3075

Mandoo's original East 32nd Street Little Korea branch is famous for its dumplings, and if the new downtown restaurant were judged on the merits of its vegetarian dumplings alone, Mandoo Bar would be a 4-star winner. Not even the dim sum palaces of Chinatown can top these. The rest of the surprisingly veggie-friendly Korean menu and the trendy but sterile decor fall short of the dumplings' impeccably high standards. Pumpkin Noodles, served in a tomato-coconut-dill sauce, can't compete with the same dish served at Franchia. Specialty dishes such as Mushroom Bokum are satisfying, but nothing more than ordinary stir-fries. The good news is that the mandoo (Korean for "dumplings") are available in both appetizer- and entrée-sized servings. Head to Mandoo Bar just for boiled and pan-fried veggie dumplings, and do so often. Main dishes from $7 to $14.

FULL MENU WITH VEGETARIAN AND VEGAN CHOICES

★★ / $$

91. Mangez Avec Moi

71-73 West Broadway
(between Warren and Murray Streets)
New York, NY 10007
212.385.0008; www.mangezavecmoi.com

PAN-ASIAN

Hours:	Mon-Fri noon to 10:00 p.m.
	Sat-Sun 11:30 a.m. to 10:00 p.m.
Payment:	Credit cards
Alcohol:	Beer
Atmosphere:	Casual dining

Don't bother trying to pinpoint the cuisine at Mangez Avec Moi. You'll find Vietnamese noodles, Thai curries, Chinese stir-fries, Japanese teriyaki, and a few dishes that seem to defy definition altogether. You'll also find a substantial number of meatless dishes, something that's quite unique for this financial district location. Add to that the bargain specials, and it comes as no surprise that this restaurant is packed during lunch hour. Arrive early if you want any chance of getting a table. Though nothing stands out as a clear winner, the food is reliably good and satisfying. For appetizers, choose the Crispy Tofu with Spicy Sauce over the misleading Sticky Rice Pancake (not a pancake at all). As for entrées, Crispy Tofu with Ginger and Scallions is slightly tangy and packed with tofu chunks. One thing is for sure— you won't leave hungry. Main dishes from $7 to $8.

**FULL MENU WITH VEGETARIAN
AND VEGAN CHOICES**

★★ / $

92. Mangia

50 West 57th Street
(between Fifth and Sixth Avenues)
New York, NY 10019
212.582.5882; www.mangiatogo.com

AMERICAN, ITALIAN

Hours:	Mon-Fri 7:30 a.m. to 8:00 p.m.
	Sat 10:00 a.m. to 6:00 p.m.
Payment:	Credit cards
Alcohol:	No
Atmosphere:	Counter service with casual seating

Other locations:
 40 Wall Street (between William and Broad Streets), New York, NY 10015, 212.425.4040;
 16 East 48th Street (between Fifth and Madison Avenues), New York, NY 10017, 212.754.7600;

22 West 23rd Street (between Fifth and Sixth Avenues),
New York, NY 10011, 212.647.0200

Take one look at the mouthwatering sandwich and
dessert counter near the entrance at Mangia and you're
hooked—this is no ordinary gourmet deli. Though the
convenient, premade sandwiches are tempting, filled
with salad-like ingredients such as marinated arti-
chokes, feta cheese, sun-dried tomatoes, broccoli rabe,
roasted peppers, and more, you should force yourself to
explore the expansive space. Visit the hot and cold buffet table for roasted vegetables, pasta dishes, and cold
salads, or wander to the rear where you'll find the pizza
ovens. Ask about daily specials, heated fresh to order, or
try one of the hot, pressed panini sandwiches such as
Gruyere and Arugula. There are meatless soups as well,
though the choices change daily. Besides the crowds,
the one complaint might be about the prices. Though
reasonable for 57th Street, the sandwiches are on the
small side for the money. Main dishes from $7 to $9.

FULL MENU WITH VEGETARIAN
AND VEGAN CHOICES

★★★ / $$

93. Meskerem

124 Macdougal Street
(between West 3rd and Bleecker Streets)
New York, NY 10012
212.777.8111

ETHIOPIAN

Hours:	noon to midnight
Payment:	Credit cards
Alcohol:	Wine and beer
Atmosphere:	Casual dining

Other Locations:
  164 Amsterdam Avenue, New York, NY 10023,
    212.799.2501;
  468 West 47th Street (between Ninth and Tenth Avenues),
    New York, NY 10036, 212.664.0520

Be warned that rumors of how great the food is at
Meskerem have spread wide and far, and this relatively
small restaurant is almost always packed with loyal
fans. If you've never tried Ethiopian food before, then
you should know that no utensils are used when dining.
You tear off a piece of the fairly bitter-tasting and very
soft flatbread and "scoop" up some of your entrée with
you hands. You should also be warned that many of
the dishes are quite spicy. For vegetarians, dining at

Meskerem is very easy. You sit down and ask for the vegetarian combo plate. You could order a single dish or two, but what fun would that be? A huge platter soon arrives with two types of lentils (one spicy, one not), a chickpea dish, two vegetable dishes, and plenty of bread. It's so dark inside, you may not be able to see what you're eating, but it won't matter because it's all fantastic. Just have plenty of beer or water handy. Entrees from $10 to $13.

FULL MENU WITH VEGETARIAN CHOICES

★★ / $$
94. Mirchi

29 Seventh Avenue South
(between Morton and Bedford Streets)
New York, NY 10014;
212.414.0931; www.mirchiny.com

INDIAN

Hours:	Sun-Thu noon to 11:00 p.m.
	Fri-Sat noon to midnight
Payment:	Credit cards
Alcohol:	Full bar
Atmosphere:	Casual dining

Unlike most Indian restaurants, the vegetarian choices at Mirchi are a bit hidden on the menu. Upon close inspection, you'll find that it's very vegetarian friendly, and more than half the choices at the bargain lunch buffet are meat-free as well. Not that there is anything wrong with the food, but the best thing about Mirchi may be the decor. There aren't many Indian restaurants in the city that look this funky, featuring a purple-and-green color scheme and bold, modern lines. See if you can score one of the tables up front—the floor-to-ceiling windows turn out to the street, making it great for people-watching in this popular West Village neighborhood. Like most Manhattan Indian restaurants, the curries are on the mild side. All of the standards are here, from Malai Kofta to Palak Panir, with a few more unique dishes tossed in, like Hyderabadi Baingan (stuffed baby eggplant in a sesame-coconut sauce). Main dishes from $10 to $12.

**FULL MENU WITH VEGETARIAN
AND VEGAN CHOICES**

★★★ / $

95. Miriam's

SW corner of West 46th Street and Sixth Avenue
New York, NY

ISRAELI, MIDDLE EASTERN

Hours:	Mon-Thu 11:00 a.m. to 5:00 p.m.
	Fri 11:00 a.m. to 2:30 p.m.
Payment:	Cash only
Alcohol:	No
Atmosphere:	Take-out cart service only

Bragging rights for NYC's top falafel remain up for grabs, but Miriam's signage declares them the winner. They may just be right, as long as you like your food on the spicy side. Even if it's a bit of a trek, you owe it to yourself to venture over to the busy corner of 46th and Sixth and brave the crowds. There's always a line at Miriam's—the good food here is no secret. Arrive early because they have run out of food on occasion, a testament to their popularity. When they ask if you want hot sauce on your falafel, be sure to answer yes. It takes a few bites to gain an appreciation for this sandwich, then the spicy heat kicks in, and you have to keep reminding yourself that this spectacular sandwich was just served off a street cart. If you're looking for something mild, try Moshe's (another cart) just across Sixth Avenue. Sandwiches from $4 to $6.

**KOSHER MENU WITH VEGETARIAN
AND VEGAN CHOICES**

★★ / $$

96. Montien

90 Third Avenue
(between East 12th and East 13th Streets)
New York, NY 10003
212.475.6814

THAI

Hours:	Mon-Thu & Sun noon to 11:00 p.m.
	Fri-Sat noon to midnight
Payment:	Credit cards
Alcohol:	Full bar
Atmosphere:	Casual dining

Though veggie friendly, Montien is certainly not the flashiest Thai restaurant downtown. It's clean and comfortable but, despite some pretty photos adorning the walls, a little nondescript. The food is on par with the decor—simple and unfussy home-style Thai cooking. In the case of the freshly fried Tofu Tod and the spicy-sweet dipping sauce or the nicely spiced Pad Thai, that's a good thing. Curries won't wow you, but they're reliable as well. Pad Sea Ew, on the other hand, is bland and dry. Elsewhere you might find this broad-noodle dish served with a rich gravy, but here it's dry and overly peppery. Montien is up against some stiff competition in the neighborhood. Style mavens may want to eat at nearby Spice, but for something more low key, Montien is worth a try. Main dishes from $10 to $12.

FULL MENU WITH VEGETARIAN

AND VEGAN CHOICES

★★ / $

97. Moshe's Falafel

SE corner of West 46th Street and Sixth Avenue
New York, NY

ISRAELI, MIDDLE EASTERN

Hours:	Mon-Thu 11:00 a.m. to 5:00 p.m.
	Fri 11:00 a.m. to 3:00 p.m.
Payment:	Cash only
Alcohol:	No
Atmosphere:	Take-out cart service only

Just when you think you've seen it all in the search for the ultimate falafel, along comes Moshe's. It's just one of many lunch carts on the remarkably busy corner of 46th and Sixth. Lines are omnipresent but move fast. Besides daily soup specials, all they serve is falafel. If you don't specify the size, they'll serve you a monster-sized sandwich, so bring your appetite. Whole pickles and big chunks of tomatoes are stuffed inside, but it's the falafel that makes this sandwich so unique. Forget about those dark green and crusty balls you get elsewhere—here the falafel is very lightly colored, slightly crispy on the outside, and evenly soft but never mushy on the inside. Even if you ask for hot sauce, this is still a mildly spiced sandwich. Though falafel purists (if there are such people) may turn up their noses, Moshe's is definitely worth trying. Sandwiches from $4 to $6.

KOSHER VEGAN

★★ / $$

98. Namaskaar

337A West Broadway (at Grand Street)
New York, NY 10013
212.625.1112; www.namaskaar.com

INDIAN

Hours:	Daily noon to 3:00 p.m.,
	5:30 p.m. to 11:00 p.m.
Payment:	Credit cards
Alcohol:	Full bar
Atmosphere:	Casual to mid-scale dining

Other locations:

123 Mall at IV, Route 4 West, Paramus, NJ 07652,
201.342.8868

Affordable vegetarian meals are tough to come by in trendy
Soho, perhaps explaining why reasonably priced Namaskaar
comes as such a pleasant surprise, that is until you actually
sit down. The dining room upstairs, isolated from the hip
Soho vibe, is pretty, but nothing about it seems Indian;
maybe that's intentional. If you manage to actually receive
the dishes that you ordered and if your bread is served
before you're halfway done with your entrée, consider your-
self lucky. The rude service is shameful because the food,
besides the bland paneer (cheese) dishes, is well prepared.
Papri Chaat (potatoes, chickpeas, yogurt, and chutney) is
tangy and spicy, and the mashed Eggplant Bhartha is a
pleasant change of pace from what you can get at most
Indian restaurants. Main dishes from $10 to $11.

**FULL MENU WITH VEGETARIAN
AND VEGAN CHOICES**

★★★ / $$

99. New Green Bo

66 Bayard Street
(between Mott and Elizabeth Streets)
New York, NY 10013
212.625.2359

CHINESE

Hours:	Daily 11:00 a.m. to midnight
Payment:	Cash only
Alcohol:	No
Atmosphere:	Casual dining

From the looks of the crowds at lunch and dinner
hours, you'd think that they were giving away the food
for free. It's no secret that New Green Bo serves some
of the best Shanghai-style Chinese food in town, but

don't let the name fool you—New Green Bo isn't nearly as "green" as it implies, though there are dozens of veggie choices. Dim sum is particularly popular here, and vegetarians won't be disappointed. Choose from Vegetable Shu-Mei, Vegetable Buns, Steamed Vegetable Dumplings, and more. Unlike anything you'll try elsewhere, the Bean Curd Puff with Shanghai Cabbage (bok choy) is a house specialty, and Ma Po Bean Curd, ordinarily laced with minced pork, is meat-free here. In addition to dishes like Eggplant with Garlic Sauce or Sautéed Water Spinach, countless meat-free noodle dishes are offered, from pan-fried to flat and wide chow fun noodles. Main dishes from $6 to $12.

FULL MENU WITH AMPLE VEGETARIAN AND VEGAN CHOICES

★★★ / $$

100. Ollie's Noodle Shop and Grille

200 West 44th Street
(between Broadway and Eighth Avenue)
New York, NY 10036
212.921.5988

CHINESE

Hours:	Mon-Thu 11:30 a.m. to midnight
	Fri-Sat 11:30 a.m. to 1:00 a.m.
	Sun 11:30 a.m. to 11:30 p.m.
Payment:	Credit cards
Alcohol:	Beer and wine
Atmosphere:	Casual dining

Other locations:
2235 Broadway (between West 79th and 80th Streets), New York, NY 10024, 212.362.3712;
1991 Broadway (between West 67th and West 68th Streets), New York, NY 10023, 212.595.8181;
2957 Broadway (at West 116th Street), New York, NY 10025, 212. 932.3300

Depending on whom you ask, Ollie's may be a little underrated. When it comes to Chinese food, most full-menu restaurants don't put a lot of effort into the meatless dishes. On the other hand, not only does Ollie's offer dozens of veggie options, but they're really tasty too. It may not be the trendiest restaurant in town, though the contemporary diner-style decor may appeal to some, and the food may not be fussy or "spiritual" like nearby Zen Palate, but you may just find a dish (or two or three) that you really enjoy. If you work in the Times Square area (or nearby one of the other three locations), then it's all the better. Plus, Ollie's is a great place to visit for a quick bite before or after a Broadway show. You won't try a better veggie General Tso's anywhere. For another treat, order the green-colored Cold Spinach Noodles in Sesame Sauce. Main dishes from $6 to $13.

FULL MENU WITH AMPLE VEGETARIAN AND VEGAN CHOICES

★★★ / $$

101. The Organic Grill

123 First Avenue
(between St. Mark's Place and East 7th Street)
New York, NY 10003
212.477.7177; www.theorganicgrill.com

AMERICAN, MULTIETHNIC

Hours:	Mon-Thu noon to 10:00 p.m.
	Fri noon to 11:00 p.m.
	Sat 10:00 a.m. to 11:00 p.m.
	Sun 10:00 a.m. to 10:00 p.m.
Payment:	Credit cards
Alcohol:	Beer and wine
Atmosphere:	Casual dining

It's easy to understand why the Organic Grill is so crowded on the weekends—everything about dining here is pleasant. Country-style benches, soft purple and pink colors inside, wood tables, an entirely old-fashioned feel, and friendly waitservice give you the feeling that you're anywhere but in New York City. Though entrée prices might seem steep, the quality of the food is very high, and there aren't many places in town with such creative meatless fare. For a better deal, stick with the terrific sandwiches, like the BBQ Seitan Sandwich topped with red onions. The Grilled Tofu Sandwich is another winner, served with roasted garlic aioli on toasted bread and a side of home fries. If you've been disappointed by soggy tofu sandwiches before, then you owe it to yourself to visit the Organic Grill. Don't forget to ask for a side of the garlicky sautéed greens. Main dishes from $8 to $14.

KOSHER VEGETARIAN WITH VEGAN CHOICES

★★ / $$

102. Organic Harvest Cafe

253 East 53rd Street
(between Second and Third Avenues)
New York, NY 10022
212.421.6444; www.organicharvestcafe.com

MULTIETHNIC

Hours:	Mon-Fri 11:00 a.m. to 10:00 p.m.
	Sat-Sun noon to 9:00 p.m.
Payment:	Credit cards
Alcohol:	No
Atmosphere:	Counter service with limited casual seating

Midtown is overrun with "gourmet" sandwich shops with little to offer vegetarians, possibly explaining why the lines are so long at Organic Harvest Cafe during lunch hour. Finally vegetarian office workers can get freshly made meatless meals. If you're in a rush, you might want to eat elsewhere, and with only three tables, you should plan on taking your food to go. Forget about chewy and lifeless veggie burgers served elsewhere—the Harvest Soy Burger is soft and satisfying, like it was made by hand just for you. Seitan Enchiladas are mildly spiced and served with a medley of vegetables, tofu sour cream, and a tomato-coriander sauce. Daily soup specials, wraps, salads, and appetizers like vegetarian dumplings are offered as well. The only real complaint is about the prices. Even the reduced-price lunch specials seem expensive. Apparently quality doesn't come cheap. Main dishes from $8 to $12.

**FULL MENU WITH MOSTLY VEGETARIAN
AND VEGAN OFFERINGS**

★★ / $$

103. Our Kitchen

520 East 14th Street (between Avenues A and B)
New York, NY 10009
212.677.8018

CHINESE

Hours:	Mon-Sat 11:00 a.m. to 11:00 p.m.
	Sun noon to midnight
Payment:	Credit cards
Alcohol:	No
Atmosphere:	Casual dining

Bordering the Gramercy area and the East Village, the far east end of 14th Street is nondescript at best, so Our Kitchen, with its bamboo-themed decor, is a nice bit of refuge from an otherwise unappealing block. Nearly every dish is offered in a meatless version, i.e., veggie pork, veggie beef, veggie chicken. Just be careful when you order—if you point to Beef with Black Bean Sauce on the extensive menu, you could end up with the meat version if you aren't specific. Avoid the hard and chewy faux-shrimp dishes. Veggie Beef with Garlic Sauce has a nice texture, but it's overwhelmed with piles of bell peppers and celery. Veggie Chicken with Sweet & Sour Sauce tastes great, but health nuts won't appreciate the battered and fried texture. Our Kitchen is a reliable place for a quick meal or takeout on your way home, but not worth going out of your way for. Main dishes from $5 to $10.

FULL MENU WITH AMPLE VEGETARIAN AND VEGAN CHOICES

★★ / $$
104. Ozu

> 566 Amsterdam Avenue
> (between West 87th and West 88th Streets)
> New York, NY 10024
> 212.787.8316
>
> **JAPANESE**

Hours:	Mon-Sat 11:30 a.m. to 10:30 p.m.
	Sun 11:30 a.m. to 10:00 a.m.
Payment:	Credit cards
Alcohol:	Wine and beer
Atmosphere:	Casual dining

Next door to the Upper West Side branch of raw-food eatery Quintessence, Ozu is yet another Japanese restaurant serving both vegan and seafood dishes. Unfortunately, it lacks the charm (and friendly wait-staff) of nearby Mana, possibly explaining why Ozu seems to attract so many solo diners at lunch hour. Check the wall for loads of daily specials. The oversized Ozu Special Noodles features rice noodles and tofu mashed up and mixed into the dish. It's a great way to get some extra protein, even if you're not a big fan of tofu. Stick with the multitude of grain and noodle dishes when ordering, just to be safe, because more inventive-sounding fare like the Lotus Root Sandwich appetizer can be disappointing. Main dishes from $8 to $11.

MOSTLY VEGAN WITH SEAFOOD CHOICES

★★ / $$

105. Paquitos

143 First Avenue
(St. Mark's Place and East 9th Street)
New York, NY 10003
212.674.2071

MEXICAN

Hours:	Daily 11:00 a.m. to 11:30 p.m.
Payment:	Credit cards
Alcohol:	Full bar
Atmosphere:	Casual dining with separate take-out entrance

Here is all the proof you need that New York City is the wrong place to come for Tex-Mex food. Paquitos is reliable and affordable, with ample meatless offerings, but if you like your Mexican food with a little spice to it, you'll need to look elsewhere. Upon seating, you're greeted with complimentary tortilla chips and what may qualify as the blandest salsa on the planet. Entrées like Spinach Enchiladas or the Acapulco Burrito aren't much different. This is mildly spiced fare, satisfying and simply prepared. The decor is quite pleasant and comfortable, with lots of exposed brick, tiled floors, and faux-adobe textured walls, and the back garden area is a real treat when the weather is nice. Avoid the take-out entrance next door. Even though the prices are a bit cheaper (for the exact same dishes), it's crowded, the service is painfully slow, and the food just isn't well suited for transporting. Main dishes from $4 to $7.

**FULL MENU WITH VEGETARIAN
AND VEGAN CHOICES**

★★ / $$

106. Pat Pong

93 East 7th Street
(between First Avenue and Avenue A)
New York, NY 10009;
212.505.6454

THAI

Hours:	Sun-Thu 4:00 p.m. to 11:00 p.m.
	Fri-Sat 4:00 p.m. to midnight
Payment:	Credit cards
Alcohol:	Wine and beer
Atmosphere:	Casual dining

This sister restaurant to Chaa Chaa on East 13th Street hasn't quite gotten it straight. The take-out menu says "vegetarian friendly," and yet the dine-in menu lists almost no meatless dishes. If you ask the waiter for clarification, they'll explain that just about any dish on the menu can be made with tofu, upon request. You have to wonder how many veggie customers overlooked Pat Pong without bothering to inquire. The chef hasn't gotten things quite right either. Panang Curry with tofu is disappointing, and any Thai restaurant that can't get their curries right is hardly worth reviewing, but the noodle dishes, on the other hand, are well done. Pad See Ewe features Chinese broccoli and shiitake mushrooms, and is bursting with flavor. The Potato Curry Puff appetizer is a flaky treat. It's a cozy and cute restaurant, worth a try, but you've been warned. Main dishes $9.

FULL MENU WITH VEGETARIAN CHOICES

★★ / $$

107. Peep

177 Prince Street
(between Thompson and Sullivan Streets)
New York, NY 10012
212.254.7337; www.peepsoho.net

THAI

Hours:	Sun-Thu 11:00 a.m. to midnight
	Fri-Sat 11:00 a.m. to 1:00 a.m.
Payment:	Credit cards
Alcohol:	Full bar
Atmosphere:	Stylish, casual dining

With mirrored ceilings, a super-chic bar area, and funky light fixtures, Peep is just as stylish as many of the nearby Soho fashion boutiques. It's too bad the owners blew their budget on the restaurant design and had so little left to invest in the kitchen staff. With one-way mirrors that allow patrons in the restrooms to "spy" on the dining room, does anyone really come here for the food anyway? Surprisingly, vegetarian options are plentiful, particularly during lunch hour—nearly every entrée is available with a choice of tofu. Though everything looks gorgeous on the plate, dishes are hit or miss. While the Basil Dish is tasty, if not addictive, the peanuty Massaman Curry is exceptionally dull. Don't be shocked if your Spinach Dumplings are stale, and beware of hidden meat when ordering. The menu fails to mention that the Semolina Fritters contain shrimp. Main dishes from $9 to $10.

**FULL MENU WITH VEGETARIAN
AND VEGAN CHOICES**

★★★ / $

108. Pommes Frites

123 Second Avenue
(East 7th Street and St. Mark's Place)
New York, NY 10003
212.674.1234; www.pommesfrites.ws

AMERICAN

Hours:	Sun-Thu 11:30 a.m. to 1:00 a.m.
	Fri-Sat 11:30 a.m. to 2:00 a.m.
Payment:	Cash only
Alcohol:	No
Atmosphere:	Take-out service with limited seating

Made from freshly cut potatoes and twice-fried for perfect texture, fries just don't get any better than this. Though comparisons have been made to B. Frites in midtown, the East Village's Pommes Frites is the hands-down winner—nothing else comes close. All they serve are Belgian-style fries; you won't find burgers (or anything else) on the menu. Seating is very limited, so take your over-stuffed paper cone container to go. There's no need for dipping because they'll carefully layer your choice of sauces in with the fries. And what a choice of sauces: European-style mayonnaise, Curry Ketchup, Peanut Satay Sauce, Dijon Garlic Mustard, Pesto Mayo, and countless more. If you can't make up your mind, the friendly staff is sure to offer you samples. The "Especial" is highly recommended—frite sauce, ketchup, and fresh onions. Fries from $4 to $7.

VEGETARIAN WITH VEGAN CHOICES

★★★ / $$

109. Pongal

110 Lexington Avenue
(between East 27th and East 28th streets)
New York, NY 10016
212.696.9458

INDIAN

Hours:	Mon 5:00 p.m. to 10:00 p.m.
	Tue-Fri noon to 3:00 p.m.,
	5:00 p.m. to 10:00 p.m.
	Sat-Sun noon to 10:00 p.m.
Payment:	Credit cards
Alcohol:	No
Atmosphere:	Stylish, casual to mid-scale dining

Pongal is a longtime favorite for its southern Indian vegetarian fare, and it's easy to understand why. Appetizers like samosas, puffed white iddly cakes, and vada (a lentil-flour fried donut) may be the best in Curry Hill. Just be sure to leave room for not-too-spicy entrées like Malai Kofta (vegetable fritters), all sorts of Paneers (cheese in curry sauces), and the fantastic Alu Chana, made with potatoes and chickpeas. Like most Indian restaurants in the area, the dosas and utthappams—pancake-like dishes filled with onions, potatoes, and peas—are a big draw. You tear off some with your hands and dip them in coconut chutney and soup. The stylish decor features exposed brick, earthy red accent colors, stone floors, and tasteful Hindi decorations; it's a nice place for a date and quiet conversation, but be warned that this popular restaurant fills up fast. Main dishes from $7 to $11.

KOSHER VEGETARIAN WITH VEGAN CHOICES

★ / $$

110. Poy Laung

> 210 Thompson Street
> (between Bleecker and West 3rd Streets)
> New York, NY 10012
> 212.533.7290
>
> **THAI**
>
> | | |
> |---|---|
> | **Hours:** | Mon-Thu noon to 10:30 p.m. |
> | | Fri noon to 11:00 p.m. |
> | | Sat 2:00 p.m. to 11:00 p.m. |
> | | Sun 2:00 p.m. to 10:30 p.m. |
> | **Payment:** | Credit cards |
> | **Alcohol:** | Beer and wine |
> | **Atmosphere:** | Casual dining |

Fans of Poy Laung must all be carnivores because there's no reason why a vegetarian would eat here twice. Located on a quiet street in the Village, it's charming enough with just a few tables to give it an intimate feel that's only slightly hindered by the odd assortment of theater posters lining the wall. But it's all downhill once you order. If you expect Thai food to strike a balance between salty, sweet, sour, and spicy flavors, you're in for a disappointing meal. Tofu with Basil Sauce is painfully oversalted and spicy, not to mention loaded with unpalatable onions and peppers. Vegetarian Green Curry is spicy, as it should be, but also packed with onions and just three pieces of tofu. That's unreasonable at any price. Unless you like hard, chewy bean curd, skip appetizers like Tofu Tod altogether. Better yet, eat somewhere else. Main dishes from $7 to $8.

**FULL MENU WITH VEGETARIAN
AND VEGAN CHOICES**

★★★ / $

111. Pukk

71 First Avenue
(between East 4th and East 5th Streets)
New York, NY 10003
212.253.2741/2742; www.pukknyc.com

THAI

Hours:	Sun-Thu 3:30 p.m. to 11:00 p.m.
	Fri-Sat 3:30 p.m. to midnight
Payment:	Credit cards
Alcohol:	Beer and sangria
Atmosphere:	Casual dining

This newcomer and one of the best vegetarian values in the Big Apple is sure to become a local favorite once the news spreads about their inventive but remarkably affordable menu. Pukk glows with green color, and the walls and floors (and some tables) are lined with tiles, so depending on your personal taste, it's either incredibly stylish or just a bit weird. In any case, it's a good nighttime date spot (especially if you order a bottle of the house sangria), and you'll forget all about the decor once you taste the contemporary Thai food. Order plenty of appetizers, including the Mushroom Puff, Oriental Chive Dumpling, Spicy Spring Roll and Curry Thai Pancake. Noodle dishes such as Pad Thai or Pad See Ew are always good, but the Pineapple Red Curry is an absolute delight, marrying spicy and sweet flavors so well. Entrees from $7 to $9.

VEGETARIAN WITH VEGAN CHOICES

★★★ / $

112. Punjabi Grocery and Deli

141 East 1st Street
(between First Avenue and Avenue A)
New York, NY 10003
212.533.9048

INDIAN

Hours:	Open 24 hours
Payment:	Cash
Alcohol:	No
Atmosphere:	Take-out service with standing
	room only

Maybe you've noticed the long line of cabs on this stretch alongside Houston Street and wondered what the fuss is about. Unlike the other popular spot next door, Punjabi is strictly vegetarian. It's a little unclear where all of the food behind the glass is made, because there is no apparent kitchen on the premises, your food will be reheated in a microwave oven, and there is nowhere to sit down. If you can get past all that, you're in for a treat. Order a combo plate and just point to what looks best. The saag (spinach) curry is just right, and the samosas are surprisingly fresh considering that the food just sits out for untold hours. Most of the regulars (taxi drivers) order the chickpea combo—a samosa is placed in a bowl and crushed, and then a chickpea curry is poured on top. Just keep in mind that everything here is spicier than you might be used to, especially by Manhattan standards. $4 for a large combo platter.

VEGETARIAN WITH VEGAN CHOICES

★★★★ / $$$

113. Pure Food & Wine

> 54 Irving Place
> (between East 17th and East 18th Streets)
> New York, NY 10003
> 212.477.1010; www.purefoodandwine.com
>
> **MULTIETHNIC**
>
> | | |
> |---|---|
> | **Hours:** | Sun-Mon 5:30 p.m. to 10:00 p.m. |
> | | Tue-Sat 5:30 p.m. to 11:00 p.m. |
> | **Payment:** | Credit cards |
> | **Alcohol:** | Wine and beer |
> | **Atmosphere:** | Mid-scale dining |

Other Locations:

> Pure Juice and Take Away, 125 1/2 East 17th Street (near Irving Place), New York, NY 10003, 212.477.7151

Who knew raw food could taste this good? Apparently though, food like this doesn't come cheap. Plan for a special date, dress nicely so you fit in with the stylish decor, and splurge on the tasting menu. It's very pricey, but there aren't many places like this in New York City where even strict vegans can have a transcendent culinary experience. Every one of the several courses will be a culinary delight and a bit of an adventure. They'll call the dishes things like samosas, tacos, or noodles, but the resemblance is tenuous. This is food as art, and the flavors may surprise you. Just keep your mind open to new tastes and textures, and enjoy. Pure Food & Wine is something you just have to try once for yourself, even if you thought you didn't like raw food. Surprisingly, the take-out branch around the corner is just as incredible, though it's obscenely expensive for boxed food. Entrées from $15 to $25.

RAW VEGAN MENU

★★ / $$

114. Quantum Leap

88 West 3rd Street
(between Thompson and Sullivan Streets)
New York, NY 10012
212.677.8050

MULTIETHNIC

Hours:	*Mon-Fri 11:30 a.m. to 11:00 p.m.*
	Sat 11:00 a.m. to 11:00 p.m.
	Sun 11:00 a.m. to 10:00 p.m.
Payment:	*Credit cards*
Alcohol:	*No*
Atmosphere:	*Casual dining*

When you see the veggie/fish menu, you might be quick to write this off as yet another Japanese health food restaurant, and what a mistake that would be. Yes, you'll find plenty of dumplings, tofu teriyaki, and tempura here, but Quantam Leap has so much more to offer, such as meatless Chili Fries. The world would be a better place if every vegetarian restaurant in town started serving chili fries. Veggie Cutlet Parmesan is another winner, smothered in tomato sauce and cheese. Meatless burgers are available in a variety of flavors, including Thai, Tex-Mex, Tofu-Hiziki, and Lentil-Walnut. Just keep in mind that the lunch menu and dinner menus are different, so your favorite dish may not always be available. Perfect for NYU students on a budget, the lunch menu is highly recommended. There is a weekend brunch menu as well, including quiches, omelets, whole-grain pancakes, and more. Main dishes from $6 to $10.

VEGETARIAN AND VEGAN MENU
WITH SEAFOOD CHOICES

★★★ / $$$

115. Quintessence

263 East 10th Street
(between First Avenue and Avenue A)
New York, NY 10009
646.654.1823; www.raw-q.com

MULTIETHNIC

Hours:	Daily 11:30 a.m. to 11:00 p.m.
Payment:	Credit cards
Alcohol:	No
Atmosphere:	Stylish, casual dining

Other locations:

566 Amsterdam Avenue (between West 87th and West 88th
Streets), New York, NY 10024, 212.501.9700;

353 East 78th Street (between First and Second Avenues)
10021, 212.734.0888

Quintessence is not the place for timid eaters.
Everything on the menu is raw, not to mention beauti-
fully prepared. If you appreciate the "food as art" aes-
thetic, then you're in for something special; fresh,
uncooked ingredients are bright pigments for a chef to
play with. The decor is equally appealing—lots of natu-
ral wood accents, bamboo mats on the tables, and pretty
pale green and yellow walls. Quintessence is comfortable,
casual, and hip, all at once. Appetizers are the real stars
here, like the Mini Pesto Pizette and the Chipotle Hand
Roll. Entrées sound a bit like dishes you may have tried
before—Mali Kofta, Caribbean Nut Meatballs, and Pasta
Putanesca—but the flavors are anything but familiar.
The truly innovative menu and the charming decor most
definitely make up for the quirky waitstaff, though the
high prices for the East Village location may scare away
some. Main dishes from $10 to $18.

RAW VEGAN MENU

★★ / $$

116. Radha

173 Ludlow Street
(between Houston and Stanton Streets)
New York, NY 10002
212.473.3374; www.radharestaurant.com

MULTIETHNIC

Hours:	Tue-Wed 5:00 p.m. to 11:00 p.m.
	Thu 5:00 p.m. to midnight
	Fri-Sat 5:00 p.m. to 1:00 a.m.
	Sun 11:00 a.m. to 3:00 p.m.
	and 5:00 p.m. to 11:00 p.m.
Payment:	Credit cards
Alcohol:	Full bar
Atmosphere:	Casual dining

In the bustling Lower East Side, Radha appears to be a refuge from the crowds and nearby meat havens like Katz's Deli and is a popular date spot, good for quiet conversation. The menu reads well, but you should probably be suspicious any time you see tortillas, Thai curry, pasta primavera and barbecue all listed together. Appetizers are generally heavy, and though it seems nearly absurd to pay $8.95 for a plate of fried soy fish sticks, unfortunately that might be the highlight of your meal. The portions are generous, a good thing since the prices are moderately high. The real problem at Radha is that the menu is overambitous. The stir-fried noodle dish Asian Temptation is satisfying, but not memorable. Barbecued Tofu will fill you up, but may leave you craving something more exciting. Entrees from $10 to $13.

VEGETARIAN WITH MANY VEGAN CHOICES

★★ / $

117. Rainbow Falafel & Shawarma

26 East 17th Street
(between Broadway and Fifth Avenue)
New York, NY 10003
212.691.8641

MIDDLE EASTERN

Hours:	Daily 8:00 a.m. to 7:00 p.m.
Payment:	Cash only
Alcohol:	No
Atmosphere:	Take-out service only

Anyone who has ever wandered down East 17th Street during lunch hour has probably wondered about the enormous line at this take-out falafel joint. In a city overrun with Middle Eastern restaurants, this one no bigger than a walk-in closet, the only seating is down the block in Union Square Park. Rest assured that the line moves fast. Rainbow makes falafel, baba ganoush, hummus, stuffed grape leaves, and not much more. Your only decision is whether you want it on a pita or on a platter, and you can't go wrong. Mamoun's on Macdougal may be the king of downtown falafel, but Rainbow comes in a close second. They're making sandwiches fast enough to keep the crowds moving, so the food has to be fresh. For a change of pace, try the enjoyable fried eggplant or fried cauliflower sandwiches. Sandwiches and platters from $4 to $8.

FULL MENU WITH MOSTLY VEGETARIAN AND VEGAN CHOICES

★★★ / $$

118. Red Bamboo Vegetarian Soul Café

140 West 4th Street
(between Macdougal Street and Sixth Avenue)
New York, NY 10012
212.260.1212; www.redbamboo-nyc.com

AMERICAN, MULTIETHNIC

Hours:	*Mon-Fri 12:30 p.m. to midnight*
	Sat-Sun noon to midnight
Payment:	*Credit cards*
Alcohol:	*Wine and beer*
Atmosphere:	*Stylish, casual dining*

Rumors about Red Bamboo's creative vegetarian menu are obviously widespread—there's almost always a wait for a table during peak dinner hours. As if great food isn't enough, the dining room is both romantic and stylish, a great spot to bring someone you want to impress. Though it might sound Chinese from the name, Red Bamboo has a lot more to offer, from Creole Soul Chicken to Honey Lemon Catfish. The drool-inducing Chicken Parmesan is thoughtfully served with your choice of veggie or dairy mozzarella cheese and garlic toast. Vegans will appreciate that any dishes made with dairy are so noted on the menu. Even if you've been turned off by mock-meat stir-fries in the past, the Citrus Beef with Asparagus may win your affection—it's so good, you might even be able to convert a few nonveggie friends. Main dishes from $7 to $13.

VEGETARIAN WITH VEGAN CHOICES

★★ / $

119. Rice

227 Mott Street
(between Prince and Spring Streets)
New York, NY 10012
212.226.5775; www.riceny.com

MULTIETHNIC

Hours:	Daily noon to midnight
Payment:	Cash only
Alcohol:	Beer
Atmosphere:	Hip, casual dining with separate take-out entrance

Other locations:

81 Washington Street (near Front Street), Dumbo,
   Brooklyn, NY 11201, 718.222.9880;
118 Lexington Avenue, New York, NY 10016, 212.686.5400;
166 DeKalb Avenue (at Cumberland Street), Fort Green,
   Brooklyn, NY 11217, 718.858.2700

This moody, stylish restaurant fits right in with the hip
boutiques of Nolita, the neighborhood just east of Soho.
Rice is usually crowded with fashion mavens taking a
break from their shopping to sample some of the most
unique food in the area. Don't worry if you can't get a
seat, because there is a separate take-out counter right
next door. As the name implies, the specialty here is rice.
Five basic varieties are available—the Thai Black Rice is
an absolute winner—as well as five "special rices" like
Green Rice cooked with cilantro, parsley, spinach, and
pine nuts. There are Carrot and Spinach Rice Balls as
well, served with an addictive tomato-cumin sauce.
Besides the rice, you're sure to enjoy the Vegetarian
Meatballs, available with your choice of either sweet
chili or spicy chili sauce. Honestly, the appetizers are so
good, you might want to skip the entrées altogether.
Main dishes from $4 to $10.

**FULL MENU WITH VEGETARIAN
AND VEGAN CHOICES**

★★★ / $$

120. Risotteria

270 Bleecker Street
(between Sixth and Seventh Avenues)
New York, NY 10014
212.924.6664; www.risotteria.com

ITALIAN

Hours:	Daily noon to 11:00 p.m.
Payment:	Credit cards
Alcohol:	Beer and wine
Atmosphere:	Casual dining

As the name implies, cozy Risotteria's specialty is risotto, a creamy, slow-cooked Italian rice dish. If you've never tried it before, risotto is comfort food at its best. Strictly vegetarian risottos are listed separately on the menu, with fantastic choices such as Spinach and Roasted Red Pepper or Gorgonzola Cheese and Toasted Walnuts. As the staff is quick to point out, there are some vegetable dishes served here that are made with chicken stock, so check the menu carefully for those marked with a V. Gluten-free dishes are conveniently marked on the menu as well. If you or your guests are in the mood for something else, you'll find well-prepared panini (grilled sandwiches), thin Neapolitan-style pizzas, and salads as well. With so many great choices, for the best experience try ordering both a risotto and a pizza, like Mozarella Cheese, Asparagus, and Truffle Oil, and share with friends. Main dishes from $9 to $12.

**FULL MENU WITH VEGETARIAN
AND VEGAN CHOICES**

★★ / $

121. Ruben's Empanadas

122 First Avenue
(between St. Mark's Place and East 7th Street)
New York, NY 10009
212.334.3351

MULTIETHNIC

Hours:	8:00 a.m. to 7:45 p.m.
Payment:	Cash only
Alcohol:	No
Atmosphere:	Take-out service with limited seating

Other locations:
505 Broome Street, New York, NY 10013, 212.979.0172;
15 Bridge Street, New York, NY 10004, 212.509.3825

Sure there are plenty of meat-filled empanadas on the menu at this East Village joint, but the value for your dollar is very high, and vegetarians are going to feel right at home. Be warned that there is something about the firm dough of these empanadas that makes you crave more. Ordering two of these satisfying pocket meals for the road is highly recommended, and one of them should definitely be the Spicy-Tofu. It's flavored just right with tomato, onion, cilantro and chile, as long as you like your food with a little bit of a heat to it. Anyone who thinks that vegetarian food is bland has obviously never been to Ruben's. The Vege-Chili empanada is also highly recommended. If you're a vegetable lover, then you're really in luck, with fillings like broccoli, corn, mushroom, potato and spinach. Empanadas from $3.50 to $4.

FULL MENU WITH VEGETARIAN AND VEGAN CHOICES

★★★ / $

122. Sacred Chow

5227 Sullivan Street
(between West 3rd and Bleecker Streets)
New York, NY 10012
212.337.0863; www.sacredchow.com

MULTIETHNIC AND BAKERY

Hours:	Mon-Fri 8:00 a.m. to 11:00 p.m.
	Sat-Sun 11:30 a.m. to 11:00 p.m.
Payment:	Credit cards
Alcohol:	Wine and beer
Atmosphere:	Casual Dining

What a difference a new location makes! Sacred Chow moved a few avenues east and transformed into what is sure to be a neighborhood favorite. Even if it's out of the way, you owe it to yourself to start eating here, often. The baked goods haven't changed—they still serve the absolute best vegan brownie—but the savory food really shines. You're going to be tempted by the affordable prices to order a lot of food, but you've been warned—portion sizes are very generous. Add to all of this that the decor is charming and the service is sincere, and you have a winner. About the food, if you enjoy creatively prepared tofu, tempeh and setain, you're going to fit right in. Order the Orange Barbecued Seitan Sub, Mama's Soy Meatball Sub, Tofu in Sunflower Pesto, Sliced Ginger Soba Noodles with Spicy Peanut Sauce, and get ready for a great meal. Tapas and sandwiches from $3 to $8.

VEGAN

★★★ / $$

123. Saigon Grill

620 Amsterdam Avenue (at West 90th Street)
New York, NY 10025
212.875.9072

VIETNAMESE

Hours:	Daily 11:00 a.m. to midnight
Payment:	Credit cards
Alcohol:	Wine and beer
Atmosphere:	Casual dining

Other locations:

1700 Second Avenue (at East 88th Street), New York, NY 10016, 212.996.4600

Finding a veggie-friendly Vietnamese restaurant is about as difficult as hailing a taxi in a rainstorm during rush hour—that is, nearly impossible. Pork has a way of showing up where you least expect it in most Vietnamese dishes, and that's why Saigon Grill comes as such a welcome surprise. Although this stylish restaurant is large, don't be surprised if it's filled to capacity, because the good food here is no secret among locals. Grilled Eggplant and Curry Okra are far from your standard Vietnamese fare; both are spicy, rich, and vibrant. Attractive plate presentations and ample portions still can't outshine the great flavors. For something more traditional, try the Bun (rice vermicelli) topped with vegetarian spring rolls. Your food is served so fast it will make your head spin, and the prices are remarkably low. If you keep your fingers crossed, maybe they'll open another location downtown! Main dishes from $6 to $7.

FULL MENU WITH VEGETARIAN
AND VEGAN CHOICES

★★ / $$

124. Salaam Bombay

319 Greenwich Street
(between Reade and Duane Streets)
New York, NY 10013
212.226.9400; www.salaambombay.com

INDIAN

Hours:	Mon-Fri 11:30 a.m. to 3:00 p.m., 5:00 p.m. to 11:00 p.m.
	Sat-Sun noon to 3:00 p.m., 5:00 p.m. to 11:00 p.m.
Payment:	Credit cards
Alcohol:	Beer and wine
Atmosphere:	Mid-scale dining

Located within a block or two of some of NYC's finest restaurants, Salaam Bombay is decidedly elegant for an Indian restaurant. White linen tablecloths and attentive waitservice are the norm, so leave your blue jeans and sneakers at home. The prices, though not unreasonable for the nicely sized portions, are upscale as well. Fortunately the veggie dishes are the most affordable ones on the menu. From the first bite of Palak Paneer (cheese and pureed spinach), you can taste the freshness. Malai Kofta (vegetable croquettes in cream sauce) is another stand-out dish. You're going to have to travel up to Lexington Avenue's Curry Hill for really top-notch veggie Indian, but Salaam Bombay is a reliable choice if you live or work in Tribeca. Main dishes from $7 to $10.

FULL MENU WITH VEGETARIAN AND VEGAN CHOICES

★★★ / $$

125. Sapore

55 Greenwich Avenue
(at Perry Street near Seventh Avenue South)
New York, NY 10014
212.229.0551

ITALIAN

Hours:	Daily noon to midnight
Payment:	Credit cards
Alcohol:	Full bar
Atmosphere:	Casual dining

There is no shortage of home-style Italian restaurants in the West Village, so what makes this one different? For one thing, the food is so good you can always expect a crowd, and the menu choices are decidedly veggie friendly. Don't miss the Grilled Portobello Mushroom and Fontina Cheese Panini for starters. Choosing among the pastas will be difficult, but the Fettucini al Carciofi (artichokes in a pink sauce with mascarpone cheese) is a winner, as is the Penne Fiorentina, a creamy spinach sauce topped with ricotta. It's hard to go wrong at Sapore, but just to be safe, skip the ho-hum salads and oversalted soups, and order yourself a big plate of pasta. Main dishes from $6 to $12.

FULL MENU WITH VEGETARIAN AND VEGAN CHOICES

★★ / $$

126. Saravana Bhavan Dosa Hut

102 Lexington Avenue
(between East 27th and East 28th Streets)
New York, NY 10016
212.725.7466; www.dosayhutny.com

INDIAN

Hours:	Tue-Sun noon to 10:00 p.m.
	Closed Mon
Payment:	Credit cards
Alcohol:	No
Atmosphere:	Casual dining

Dosa Hut, as it's more commonly known and bearing no relation to its Flushing-based namesake, located just steps away from Pongal, just can't compete with its neighbors with respect to atmosphere. This is not the place to bring your parents when they're in town, let alone a hot date you want to impress. As you might expect from the name, the dosas are particularly good. Mysore Masala is cooked to crispy perfection with a nicely spiced potato-onion filling served with a smartly soupy coconut chutney that's perfect for dunking. Curries such as the runny Palak Paneer are unfortunately not quite up to the level of the dosas. They're not necessarily bad, but if you love the thick and rich curries at the neighboring restaurants, you might be a little disappointed. Stick with the dosas just to be safe. Main dishes from $6 to $11.

KOSHER VEGETARIAN WITH VEGAN CHOICES

★★★ / $$

127. Sea

75 Second Avenue
(between East 4th and East 5th Streets)
New York, NY 10003
212.228.5505; www.spicenyc.net

THAI

Hours:	Sun-Thu 11:30 a.m. to 11:00 p.m.
	Fri-Sat 11:30 a.m. to 1:00 a.m.
Payment:	Credit cards
Alcohol:	Full bar
Atmosphere:	Stylish, casual dining

Other locations:

114 North 6th Street (between Berry and Wythe Streets),
Williamsburg, Brooklyn, NY 11211, 718.834.8850

See page 154 for details.

FULL MENU WITH AMPLE VEGETARIAN
AND VEGAN CHOICES

★★ / $

128. Slice

1413 Second Avenue
(between East 73rd and East 74th Streets)
New York, NY 10021
212.249.4353; www.sliceperfect.com

PIZZERIA

Hours:	Sun-Thu 11:00 a.m. to 11:00 p.m.
	Fri-Sat 11:00 a.m. to 1:00 p.m.
Payment:	Credit cards
Alcohol:	No
Atmosphere:	Take-out service with limited seating

The menu at Slice is one small step away from being completely vegetarian, and it's a little unclear why they don't just make the leap and go totally veggie. But this review may be getting ahead of itself, because things are a bit peculiar at this "pizzeria." First, forget what you know about pizza. Each slice is cut into 4 mini wedges, making it perfect for snacking with friends. The menu descriptions sound spectacular, even if the names—Dunce, Beginner, Intermediate, etc.—may be misleading. Hardcore herbivores may be inclined to order the Master, made with crumbled tofu and jalapeños on a honey whole wheat crust, but it's not nearly as exciting as it sounds. You're better off trying the Skilled, topped with black olives, eggplant and a sundried tomato pesto sauce. But considering the steep prices, you may be better off dining somewhere else. Pizza slices from $3.50 to $5.

FULL MENU WITH VEGETARIAN CHOICES

★★ / $

129. 'Snice

45 Eighth Avenue (at West 4th Street)
New York, NY 10014
212.645.0310

AMERICAN AND MULTIETHNIC

Hours:	Mon-Fri 7:30 a.m. to 10:30 p.m.
	Sat-Sun 8:00 a.m. to 10:00 p.m.
Payment:	Cash
Alcohol:	No
Atmosphere:	Take-out service with casual seating

This is officially the most family-friendly vegetarian restaurant in New York City. You're unlikely to ever dine at 'Snice and not see at least half a dozen people with babies and young children, but it's so casual and perpetually busy, nobody seems to mind. Salads are offered, but the sandwiches are the real stars here. You'd do well by stopping in with a few friends, ordering a variety of sandwiches, and then sharing, because some of these are packed with flavor. You have to basically forget what you know about vegetarian sandwiches, the bland and lifeless things sold in so many health food stores. At 'Snice, you can count on a range of unexpected textures and flavors, from Deb's Garbage Loaf, a meat-free meatloaf, to the Tempeh Reuben, topped with Thousand Island Dressing, or the Philly-Style Seiten Sandwich, a new twist on the cheesesteak. This is comfort food with a twist. Sandwiches $7.

VEGETARIAN WITH MANY VEGAN CHOICES

★★ / $$
130. Souen

> 28 East 13th Street
> (between Fifth Avenue and University Place)
> New York, NY 10003
> 212.627.7150; www.souen.net
>
> **JAPANESE**
>
> | | |
> |---|---|
> | **Hours:** | Mon-Sat 10:00 a.m. to 11:00 p.m. |
> | | Sun 10:00 a.m. to 10:00 p.m. |
> | **Payment:** | Credit cards |
> | **Alcohol:** | Beer and wine |
> | **Atmosphere:** | Casual dining |

Other locations:
  210 Sixth Avenue (at Prince Street), New York, NY 10014, 212.807.7421

Practically a downtown landmark for vegetarians, you either love Souen or hate it. If you're looking for bold flavors and sexy atmosphere, head over to Gobo or Red Bamboo. Like most natural Japanese/seafood restaurants in the city, everything on the strictly organic menu is healthy. Even the decor is good for you—very relaxed and comfortable with lots of hanging plants near the entrance. Unfortunately, the Hijiki Seaweed Salad is bland and lifeless. Sauces are generally served on the side for calorie counters, and the trick seems to be to drown your food in the accompanying sauces if you're concerned about the taste. For example, the fried and dull Tempeh Croquettes don't have much to offer without the tofu-tahini dip. Carrot-ginger dressing brings life to steamed veggies. If you're on a restrictive diet, Souen is worth checking out. Main dishes from $8 to $13.

**MOSTLY VEGETARIAN AND VEGAN
CHOICES WITH SEAFOOD**

★★ / $

131. Soy Luck Club

115 Greenwich Avenue (at Jane Street)
New York, NY 10014
212.229.9191; www.soyluckclub.com

AMERICAN, CAFÉ

Hours:	Mon-Fri 8:30 a.m. to 9:30 p.m.
	Sat-Sun 9:30 a.m. to 9:30 p.m.
Payment:	Credit cards
Alcohol:	No
Atmosphere:	Casual dining

For a stylish and casual hangout (with wi-fi access) in
the West Village, Soy Luck Club is a winner and a great
alternative to the big chain coffee shops that have taken
over Manhattan. From the name, you might expect a
strictly vegetarian menu. Order one of the signature soy
milk drinks (served hot or cold) in flavors like honey and
ginger, dark chocolate, or vanilla and caramel, and you'll
find it in your heart to forgive them for serving poultry
and tuna. Soy shows up in all forms, not just tofu: soy
yogurt, soy mayo, soy nuts. The egg-salad-like Tofu Salad,
Avocado, and Soy Mayo sandwich stands out, if just for
the shear innovation, but for a real treat, try the
Roasted Pepper, Spinach, Basil Pesto & Swiss Panini,
grilled to perfection. Daily soup specials and creative
salads are offered as well. Sandwiches from $7 to $9.

**FULL MENU WITH VEGETARIAN
AND VEGAN CHOICES**

★★★ / $$

132. Spice

60 University Place (at East 10th Street)
New York, NY 10003
212.982.3758; www.spicenyc.net

THAI

Hours:	Mon-Fri 11:30 a.m. to 11:00 p.m.
	Sat-Sun 11:30 a.m. to midnight
Payment:	Credit cards
Alcohol:	Full bar
Atmosphere:	Stylish, casual dining

Other locations:

199 Eighth Avenue (between West 20th and West 21st
Streets), New York, NY 10011, 212.989.1116;
1411 Second Avenue (between West 73rd and West 74th
Streets), New York, NY 10021, 212.988.5348

Much like its sister restaurants, Sea and Peep, Spice is a
destination for Thai food in stylish surroundings. Twenty

or so well-prepared vegetarian dishes are offered, so it should come as no surprise that Spice now has three locations in Manhattan. It doesn't hurt that the food tastes so good either—there are a lot of ordinary Thai restaurants in the Big Apple, and this is definitely not one of them. Emerald Vegetable Dumplings are served with a vibrant black plum sauce for dipping, as are the Fresh Summer Rolls. Curry dishes are just spicy enough for anyone to enjoy. Black Noodles (broad noodles and egg in a black bean sauce) is as good as it gets. Vegetarian Pineapple Duck may be the highlight of the menu, with great textures and an even better sauce. It's hard to go wrong at Spice, and if you can score a table by the window for people-watching on University Place, it's all the better. Main dishes from $7 to $9.

FULL MENU WITH VEGETARIAN

AND VEGAN CHOICES

★★★ / $$

133. Spring Street Natural

62 Spring Street (at Lafayette Street)
New York, NY 10012
212.966.0290

MULTIETHNIC

Hours:	*Sun-Thu 11:30 a.m. to midnight*
	Fri-Sat 11:30 a.m. to 1:00 a.m.
Payment:	*Credit cards*
Alcohol:	*Full bar*
Atmosphere:	*Casual dining*

In a neighborhood where many of the fashion boutiques are no larger than walk-in closets, Spring Street Natural's cavernous dining room is something of an oddity. Even more impressive are the throngs of people who fill the place day and night. Outside seating— great for people-watching—is particularly hard to come by. Since the waitservice is abrupt at best, maybe it's the creative and satisfying meatless menu choices that have earned this restaurant such a loyal following. Start off with an appetizer like Crisp Marinated Tempeh, served with two great dipping sauces. The Grilled Portobello Sandwich with black olive mayonnaise is one of the tastiest sandwiches in the city. To satisfy a big appetite, opt for the deceptively simple-sounding Stir-Fried Organic Season Vegetables, infused with tamari, ginger, and garlic, and served over brown rice; who needs Chinatown when you can get Asian-inspired food like this? Main dishes from $8 to $13.

FULL MENU WITH VEGETARIAN

AND VEGAN CHOICES

★★ / $

134. Strictly Roots

2058 Adam Clayton Powell Jr. Boulevard
(Seventh Avenue, between West 122nd and West
123rd Streets)
New York, NY 10027
212.864.8699

CARIBBEAN

Hours:	Mon-Sat 11:00 a.m. to 10:00 p.m.
	Sun noon to 7:00 p.m.
Payment:	Credit cards
Alcohol:	No
Atmosphere:	Counter service with casual seating

Don't worry if you can't make up your mind about what
to order at this strictly vegan Harlem eatery. They serve
nothing that "crawls, walks, swims, or flies" and use
only organic ingredients, so you really can't go wrong.
The friendly staff is happy to explain the offerings, but
you're best off ordering a sampler plate—a little bit of
everything. Whatever you decide on, just be sure it
includes the sweet Fried Plantains. Entrée choices vary
day to day and might include Baked Tofu, Curry Veggie
Chicken, and Stir-Fry Gluten. Everything is mildly
spiced, but the vegetable dishes like the collard greens
just don't compare with the protein-based ones. Think
of the food here as satisfying, home-style cooking, not
to mention a terrific value. The vibe is laid-back and
very casual, a great place to check out if you happen to
be in the neighborhood. Combo plates from $6 to $8.

VEGAN

★★★ / $

135. Sullivan Street Bakery

73 Sullivan Street
(between Spring and Broome Streets)
New York, NY 10012
212.334.9435; www.sullivanstreetbakery.com

BAKERY, PIZZERIA

Hours:	Daily 7:00 a.m. to 7:00 p.m.
Payment:	Credit cards
Alcohol:	No
Atmosphere:	Counter service only, very limited seating

Other locations:

533 West 47th Street (between Tenth and Eleventh
Avenues), New York, NY 10036, 212.265.5580

You may already know about Sullivan Street Bakery's
fantastic breads and rolls, served at many of the city's

finest restaurants, but it's the entirely vegetarian pizza menu that is the real star here. There's no pepperoni or sausage in sight, nor will you find any round pizza pies piled high with mozzarella. And don't even think about asking them to heat up a slice for you. Sullivan's room-temperature, thin-crusted pizza is simplicity at its best. Pizza Bianca is topped with olive oil, fresh rosemary, salt, and nothing more. Pizza Patate is covered with thinly sliced potatoes, and Pizza Funghi is smothered with minced crimini mushrooms. These pizzas need no further adornment, and they can be downright addictive. There are seasonal pizzas as well, and the friendly staff is usually happy to give you a sample. With just a few stools and two benches outside, takeout is almost required. Pizza from $3 to $4.

VEGETARIAN WITH VEGAN CHOICES

★★ / $$

136. Suzie's

162 Bleecker Street
(between Thompson and Sullivan Streets)
New York, NY 10012
212.777.1395

CHINESE

Hours:	Mon-Thu 11:30 a.m. to 12:30 a.m.
	Fri-Sat noon to 2:00 a.m.
	Sun noon to midnight
Payment:	Credit cards
Alcohol:	Full bar
Atmosphere:	Casual dining

Conveniently located near NYU and open late on the weekends to cater to the Bleecker Street bar crowds, Suzie's has been a Village favorite for thirty years. With respect to decor, it has most Chinatown restaurants beat by a mile. Suzie's is clean and comfortable, and the etched-glass designs, Chinese artwork, and soft lighting all add a touch of elegance to the dining room. Dozens of meatless dishes are offered, and the General Tso's Vegetarian-Style Chicken is, as the menu says, a "must try." Other entrées such as Hunan-Style Vegetarian Chicken fall short—the bean curd chunks are either overcooked or stale (much like the complimentary wonton crackers). Dim sum should be avoided altogether; if you're in the mood for dumplings, head for Chinatown. Main dishes from $7 to $9.

**FULL MENU WITH VEGETARIAN
AND VEGAN CHOICES**

★★★★ / $$$

137. Tabla Bread Bar

11 Madison Avenue (at East 25th Street)
New York, NY 10010
212.889.0667

INDIAN

Hours:	*Mon-Fri noon to 11:00 p.m.*
	Sat-Sun 5:30 p.m. to 11:00 p.m.
Payment:	*Credit cards*
Alcohol:	*Full bar*
Atmosphere:	*Stylish, mid-scale dining*

While the pricier menu upstairs at Tabla is heavy on the meat offerings, the gorgeous yet hip café known as Tabla Bread Bar is very veggie friendly. Despite what you may have heard, calling this Indian food is a bit of an exaggeration, so leave any inhibitions about authentic cuisine at home. Saag Paneer Pizza is better tasting than you'd ever guess, with a thin and crispy crust. Standard breads are offered, but try the cheese-filled Cheese Kulcha and order the Tomato Kalonji chutney to go with it. Although the name sounds familiar, the hummus is far from ordinary—it's richer and more complex than anything you've tried before. Even the simple sautéed market greens are terrific. As if the impeccable waitservice wasn't good enough, eating at Tabla Bread Bar is an adventure for the palate. Order small plates and share for the best experience. Small dishes from $5 to $15.

**FULL MENU WITH AMPLE VEGETARIAN
AND VEGAN CHOICES**

★★★ / $

138. Taïm

222 Waverly Place (just off Seventh Avenue South)
New York, NY 10014
212.691.1287; www.taimnyc.com

MIDDLE EASTERN

Hours:	*noon to 10:00 p.m.*
Payment:	*Cash*
Alcohol:	*No*
Atmosphere:	*Take-out service with very limited barstool seating*

A question you don't hear very often is, what's new in the world of falafel? Taïm has the answer, though it's tucked away on a residential block, so be thankful you're reading this review. It's important to note, thankfully, that this is one of the only falafel joints in town where it doesn't reek from the smell of greasy shawarma, because Taïm is strictly vegetarian. Regular falafel is offered, but it's the roasted red pepper- and harissa- (paprika and garlic) flavored falafels that you'll want to try. The Israeli-style pita breads are puffy and soft, offered in either white or whole wheat varieties. As good as the falafel is, the Sabich (fried eggplant) is even better, served with a very zesty amba sauce on the side. And whatever you do, make sure to order the french fries with saffron aioli, a new contender for the best fries sold anywhere in Manhattan. Sandwiches and platters from $4.50 to $9.

VEGETARIAN WITH VEGAN CHOICES

★★ / $$$
139. Tamarind

41-43 East 22nd Street
(between Broadway and Park Avenue)
New York, NY 10010
212.674.7400

INDIAN

Hours:	Sun-Thu 11:00 a.m. to 2:45 p.m., 5:30 p.m. to 11:15 p.m.
	Fri-Sat 11:00 a.m. to 2:45 p.m., 5:30 p.m. to 11:45 p.m.
Payment:	Credit cards
Alcohol:	Full bar
Atmosphere:	Mid- to upscale dining

This is one restaurant where you're definitely going to need a credit card—even the basmati rice costs extra. Great for business lunches or dining out with your parents, Tamarind is upscale and elegant. It's stark white with just a few touches of Indian culture and designed to impress, so dress appropriately. Familiar dishes like Saag Paneer (pureed spinach and cheese) fall a little short of the mark, especially for the hefty price. Opt for dishes with names you don't recognize such as the zesty Achari Mushroom, unlike anything you can get on nearby Lexington Avenue. The Raj Kachori appetizer may taste familiar (chickpeas, raita, tamarind sauce), but the presentation, served inside a bread bowl, is dramatic and fun. One of the best things about Tamarind is the service; if you're sharing dishes, the staff will plate your food right at the table. Main dishes from $12 to $15.

**FULL MENU WITH VEGETARIAN
AND VEGAN CHOICES**

★★★ / $$

140. Tang Tang

> 1328 Third Avenue (at East 76th Street)
> New York, NY 10021
> 212.249.2102

> **CHINESE**

> **Hours:** Sun-Thu 11:30 a.m. to 11:00 p.m.
> Fri-Sat 11:30 a.m. to 11:15 p.m.
> **Payment:** Credit cards
> **Alcohol:** No
> **Atmosphere:** Casual dining

Tang Tang is one full-menu Chinese restaurant that knows how to make veggies feel welcome—thirty-four vegetable dishes on the first page of the menu alone, with more scattered throughout. The Upper East Side location and bargain prices make it all the more intriguing. All you really need to know is that a trip to Tang Tang without ordering the Sesame Noodles is unforgivable. They've set the standard very high, and nothing else in town comes close. Most everything on the menu is reliable as well. They serve standard-sounding Chinese fare, prepared to perfection every time. Moo Shu Vegetable, Chinese Broccoli with Bean Curd, Broccoli with Garlic Sauce—you just can't go wrong. The only question is, why would area residents order Chinese from anyplace else? Main dishes from $7 to $8.

**FULL MENU WITH AMPLE VEGETARIAN
AND VEGAN CHOICES**

★ / $

141. The Temple in the Village

> 74 West 3rd Street
> (between La Guardia Place and Thompson Street)
> New York, NY 10012
> 212.475.5670

> **MULTIETHNIC**

> **Hours:** Mon-Sat 11:00 a.m. to 9:30 p.m.
> Closed Sun
> **Payment:** Cash only
> **Alcohol:** No
> **Atmosphere:** Self-serve hot and cold buffet bar
> with casual seating area

Despite bargain basement prices and a strict vegan menu, dining at The Temple is a chore at best; subway cars during rush hour have more charm. Try closing your eyes when you serve yourself—it doesn't matter much since all of the cold entrées taste the same: bland. At least a few of the hot choices are palatable, like the BBQ tofu chunks, but that's not saying much. Flavor is apparently not the point here. Catering to vegans and anyone else on a highly restrictive diet, they thoughtfully provide exacting dietary details for every dish. If you're diabetic or hypoglycemic, you'll have no problem figuring out which choices are best for you. Need to know which dishes are high in fiber or if any are oil-free? They've got it covered. Washington Square Park is just a block away, so take your food to go. Hot and cold buffet sold by weight.

VEGAN

★★ / $$
142. Thai Angel

141 Grand Street
(between Broadway and Lafayette Streets)
New York, NY 10013
212.966.8916

THAI

Hours:	Mon-Sat 11:30 a.m. to 11:00 p.m.
	Sun noon to 11:00 p.m.
Payment:	Credit cards
Alcohol:	Wine and beer
Atmosphere:	Casual dining

Other locations:
   34-11 30th Avenue, Astoria, Queens, NY 11103,
      718.726.7029

Just a block or two away from the tacky, overlit and noisy restaurants of Chinatown, Thai Angel is a breath of fresh air. Wood accents, soft music, dim lights and candles at every table make it ideal for dinner with a special someone or a close friend. Better yet, this is one of a handful of Thai places in the city with vegetarian specialties, rather than just a choice of substituting tofu for the meat. Start off with Fried Tofu & Taro served with a sweet chili sauce. Vegetarian Duck Garlic is accurately named—after a few bites of this winner, your breath will ward off vampires (so don't forget the breath mints). There are plenty of meatless curry dishes to choose from, but if you can't take the heat, try the slightly sweet and peanuty Vegetarian Masaman Curry. Main dishes from $6 to $9.

FULL MENU WITH VEGETARIAN
AND VEGAN CHOICES

★★★ / $$

143. Thai House Cafe

> 151 Hudson Street (at Hubert Street)
> New York, NY 10013
> 212.334.1085
>
> THAI
>
> | | |
> |---|---|
> | Hours: | Mon-Sat 11:00 a.m. to 11:00 p.m. |
> | | Closed Sun |
> | Payment: | Cash only |
> | Alcohol: | Wine and beer |
> | Atmosphere: | Casual dining |

Tribeca may be home to some of the city's finest restaurants, but you're nearly out of luck if you're looking for reasonable prices, let alone vegetarian food. From the look of the huge crowds at lunchtime, it's no secret that Thai House Cafe addresses both concerns, with great-tasting food to boot. In addition to some meatless specialties, nearly every dish on the menu is available with a choice of tofu (or just veggies if you prefer), more than making up for the hurried service and lack of ambiance. Curries are rich in flavor with a kick of chile, although the spiciness can be adjusted to taste. And unlike other Thai restaurants that load the curry dishes with onions and bland peppers, Thai House opts for broccoli, green beans, peas, cabbage, and more. Another well-seasoned dish is the Vegetarian Duck, topped with julienned bamboo shoots. Main dishes from $7 to $9.

FULL MENU WITH AMPLE VEGETARIAN AND VEGAN CHOICES

★★★ / $$

144. Thali

> 28 Greenwich Avenue
> (between Sixth and Seventh Avenues)
> New York, NY 10011
> 212.367.7411
>
> INDIAN
>
> | | |
> |---|---|
> | Hours: | Daily 12:30 p.m. to 3:00 p.m., |
> | | 5:30 p.m. to 10:00 p.m. |
> | Payment: | Cash only |
> | Alcohol: | No |
> | Atmosphere: | Casual dining |

Don't blink while walking up Greenwich Avenue or you might miss Thali, a very narrow and cozy restaurant with just ten small tables. In this case, size doesn't count—Thali serves some of the best Indian food in New York City. Once you've ordered a mango lassi and appetizers (the Bombay Crepe is a work of art and tastes even better than it looks), your waiter tells you about the vegetables of the day. There are no menus, just incredible food. The fixed-price thali comes to you on a large silver tray with roti bread, basmati rice, and small bowls of lentil soup, vegetable curry, raita, chutney, and dessert. Everything is perfectly prepared, satisfying, wonderfully aromatic, spicy, sweet, and soothing. If you normally don't care for rice pudding or cucumber-tomato chutney, you haven't tried them at Thali. Fixed price, $6 lunch and $11 dinner.

VEGETARIAN

★★ / $$
145. Three of Cups

83 First Avenue (at East 5th Street)
New York, NY 10003
212.388.0059; www.threeofcupsny.com

ITALIAN

Hours:	Mon-Thu 6:00 p.m. to 1:00 a.m.
	Fri-Sat 6:00 p.m. to 2:00 a.m.
	Sun noon to 1:00 a.m.
Payment:	Credit cards
Alcohol:	Full bar
Atmosphere:	Casual dining

If you're looking for a dark, moody restaurant with ample meatless offerings, you're in luck. With the exception of the Sunday brunch, Three of Cups is only open for dinner, and the lights are turned down low, making it ideal for intimate conversation—if they'd only turn down the music a bit. A tough-to-beat, early bird dinner special includes a complimentary glass of wine and a garden salad with your entrée. Simple pastas and pizzas are the specialty here. While not necessarily memorable, everything is generously portioned and satisfying. Health nuts may want to avoid the pastas though—Penne con Finnochio (fennel and leeks) is swimming in oil. An individual-sized Artichoke Pizza is a safer bet. Just be sure to order an appetizer or salad to start because the pizzas are baked fresh to order in a wood-burning stove. Main dishes from $8 to $18.

FULL MENU WITH AMPLE VEGETARIAN
AND VEGAN CHOICES

★★★ / $$

146. Tibet Shambala

488 Amsterdam Avenue
(between West 83rd and West 84th Streets)
New York, NY 10024
212.721.1270

TIBETAN

Hours:	Daily 12:30 p.m. to 3:30 p.m.,
	5:30 p.m. to 11:00 p.m.
Payment:	Credit cards
Alcohol:	No
Atmosphere:	Casual dining

The nation of Tibet is wedged between China and India, so it should come as no surprise that the food borrows from both countries' cuisines. Where else can you find dumplings and curries on the same menu? If you've never tried Tibetan food, it might be worth a trip to the Upper West Side. The full menu, accurately described as "Tibetan home cooking," features a surprising number of vegetarian dishes. Even with attractive artwork on the walls, the decor doesn't stand out, but at these prices you can afford to bring along a few culinarily adventurous friends. Shogo Fried Dumplings filled with potatoes and onions are comforting, but the dipping sauce is incendiary. Himalayan Cauli Khatsa, assorted vegetables served in a spicy tomato sauce and served cold, is hearty and satisfying, with just enough kick to keep you reaching for the water. Main dishes from $8 to $10.

**FULL MENU WITH VEGETARIAN
AND VEGAN CHOICES**

★★ / $$

147. Tiengarden

170 Allen Street
(between Rivington and Stanton Streets)
New York, NY 10002
212.388.1364

PAN-ASIAN

Hours:	Mon-Sat noon to 10:00 p.m.
	Closed Sun
Payment:	Credit cards
Alcohol:	No
Atmosphere:	Casual dining with take-out service

For a strictly vegan menu, Tiengarden should win awards for the level of creativity. Wheat gluten, soy protein, and bean curd are served in ways you've never seen before, with a sensitive eye for healthfulness in the preparation. A little more ambiance would be nice at this Lower East Side restaurant, but don't let that keep you away. The friendly staff is happy to make recommendations if the number of selections to choose from seems a bit overwhelming. Many of the best dishes can be found on the appetizer and dim sum list, like the baked or fried Spring Rolls and the Crispy Gluten with a zesty BBQ sauce for dunking. Though well prepared and not greasy at all, fried food seems to be in overabundance on the menu. That being said, the Sesame Nuggets in sweet-and-sour sauce are a sure-fire hit. Main dishes from $6 to $12.

VEGAN

★★★ / $

148. Tiny's Giant Sandwich Shop

191 Rivington Street
(between Attorney and Ridge Streets)
New York, NY 10002
212.982.1690; www.tinysgiant.com

AMERICAN

Hours:	11:00 a.m. to 11:00 p.m.
Payment:	Cash only
Alcohol:	No
Atmosphere:	Casual dining

Consider this review to be an open letter to every other vegetarian restaurant in New York City, if not the world: please stop serving veggie burgers because nothing can possibly compare to the Big Mack Daddy at Tiny's. What's their secret? It might be the condiments, and any recently-converted vegetarians who are still craving fast-food hamburgers will probably agree after one taste. Be warned that this place isn't very big, and it fills up fast during peak hours because everybody in the Lower East Side seems to know how good the food is. If you come with a friend or two, one of you should order the Veggie Meatball Parmesan sandwich (again, possibly the best served anywhere) and the Silly Philly Cheese Steak. But don't be surprised if you start craving the Big Mack Daddy and find yourself coming back for more, often. Sandwiches from $4 to $8.

FULL MENU WITH VEGETARIAN
AND VEGAN CHOICES

★★ / $$

149. Tsampa

212 East 9th Street
(between Second and Third Avenues)
New York, NY 10003
212.614.3226

TIBETAN

Hours:	Daily 5:00 p.m. to 11:30 p.m.
Payment:	Credit cards
Alcohol:	Wine and beer
Atmosphere:	Casual dining

Tsampa takes moody lighting to extremes. You practically
need a flashlight in order to read the menu, but once
the formalities are out of the way, it's dark, quiet, and
calming. This is definitely not the place to bring young
kids or a boisterous bunch of friends. Think date
night—maybe that's why Tsampa isn't open for lunch.
Don't worry about trying to define Tibetan food. It's
Chinese-inspired with a twist, but it's the "natural food"
sign on the door that more accurately defines this
restaurant and is perhaps its downfall. The shiitake pan-
cake more closely resembles a Middle Eastern flat bread
than the greasy scallion pancakes you may know and
love. Sautéed greens (Ngo Ngopa) are light on flavor
and, much like the tofu with black bean sauce, oversalted.
Tsampa is a winner for calorie counters looking for a
romantic night out. Main dishes from $9 to $10.

**FULL MENU WITH VEGETARIAN
AND VEGAN CHOICES**

★★ / $$

150. Udipi Palace

101 Lexington Avenue
(between East 27th and East 28th Streets)
New York, NY 10016
212.889.3477

INDIAN

Hours:	Mon-Fri 11:30 a.m. to 10:00 p.m.
	Sat-Sun 11:30 a.m. to 10:30 p.m.
Payment:	Credit cards
Alcohol:	Beer and wine
Atmosphere:	Casual dining

Amid stiff competition on Lexington Avenue's Curry
Hill, Udipi Palace is struggling to compete with its
neighbors. While Pongal across the street has customers
lined up for a table, Udipi looks more like a ghost
town. Maybe it has something to do with the tacky

suburban-chic decor or the unpleasant waitservice? Prices are on par with area restaurants, but the portions are a bit lean. It's a shame because curries like Malai Kofta (vegetable fritters in a creamy sauce) are well prepared, but leave you hungry at the end of the meal. White rice is listed on the menu for three dollars, but don't be surprised if your inconsiderate waiter forgets to mention that rice is included with your entrée. If you've sampled the delicate cheese dosas at nearby Dimple, you're in for a disappointment at Udipi, unless a mushy pancake stuffed with smelly cheese sounds good to you. Main dishes from $7 to $9.

KOSHER VEGETARIAN WITH VEGAN CHOICES

★★ / $

151. Uncle Moe's Burrito and Taco Shop

14 West 19th Street
(between Fifth and Sixth Avenues)
New York, NY 10011
212.727.9400

MEXICAN

Hours:	Mon–Fri 11:30 a.m. to 9:30 p.m.
	Sat noon to 7:00 p.m.
	Closed Sun
Payment:	Credit cards
Alcohol:	No
Atmosphere:	Counter service with casual seating

Other locations:
341 Seventh Avenue (between 9th and 10th Streets), Park Slope, Brooklyn, NY 11215, 718.965.0006

The retro, diner-style decor makes Uncle Moe's a funky spot for lunch on weekdays (it's abandoned at other times of the week), but good luck finding a free table. Reasonable prices and huge portions might explain why this is one of the most popular spots in the neighborhood. Too bad the meatless offerings aren't a little more exciting. There's plenty to eat, including veggie tostadas, tacos, chalupas, burritos, enchiladas, and more, but it takes a lot of extra salsa to jazz things up. Skip the lifeless soft-shell tacos altogether. The menu's one standout is the North Beach San Francisco–Style Wrap, with marinated portobello mushrooms in a spinach tortilla. Another safe bet is to order your burrito with the veggie filling of the day, far more interesting than the standard rice and beans. Main dishes from $3 to $8.

**FULL MENU WITH VEGETARIAN
AND VEGAN CHOICES**

★★★ / $

152. Uptown Juice Bar

54 West 125th Street
(between Lenox and 5th Avenues)
New York, NY 10027
212.987.2660; www.uptownjuicebar.com

CARIBBEAN, AMERICAN

Hours:	*Daily 8:00 a.m. to 10:00 p.m.*
Payment:	*Cash only*
Alcohol:	*No*
Atmosphere:	*Counter service with casual seating*

Yes, there is a juice bar here, but it's the creative and boldly flavored vegetarian fare that are the real draw. If you rarely venture up to Harlem, this place is definitely worth the trip, because Uptown Juice Bar offers an astounding value for your vegetarian dollar. The selection can be overwhelming: soy chunks drenched in barbecue sauce, eggplant fillet smothered in tomato sauce, Cajun Tofu, and veggie meatloaf, not to mention vegetable dishes like collard greens or okra. You're best off going with a friend or two who don't mind sharing so you can try as many different dishes as possible. After you make your selection at the counter, be sure to venture to the back of the restaurant where you'll find ample seating in a pretty, atrium-like area, with artwork lining the walls. Try a dairy-free dessert when you're finished. Combo plates $6.

VEGETARIAN WITH VEGAN CHOICES

★★★★ / $$$

153. Vatan

409 Third Avenue (at East 29th Street)
New York, NY 10016
212.689.5666

INDIAN

Hours:	*Tue-Thu 5:30 p.m. to 9:00 p.m.*
	Fri-Sat 5:30 p.m. to 10:30 p.m.
	Sun 5:00 p.m. to 9:00 p.m.
Payment:	*Credit cards*
Alcohol:	*Beer*
Atmosphere:	*Casual to mid-scale dining*

No matter how many southern Indian restaurants you've tried before, Vatan sets a new standard for excellence. There are no menus and no ordering; it's a fixed price feast. Since the amazing food is no secret, reservations are recommended—try to request one of the special booths that require the removal of your shoes. The decor is a spectacle, adorned with evocative Indian artwork. The very friendly waitstaff, decked out in traditional Indian garb, first brings you a plate of appetizers, like mini samosas and pakoras. Soon after, you are presented with another huge tray of food: rice, breads, dal, raita, and vegetables. The menu varies daily, but it's safe to say that the curries are always astounding. Your waiter will practically insist that you order second and even third helpings of your favorite dishes. Save a little room for the unique dessert tray. Fixed price menu $22.

VEGETARIAN WITH VEGAN CHOICES

★★ / $$

154. Vegetarian Dim Sum House

24 Pell Street (between Doyers and Mott Streets)
New York, NY 10013
212.577.7176

CHINESE

Hours:	Daily 10:30 a.m. to 10:30 p.m.
Payment:	Cash only
Alcohol:	No
Atmosphere:	Casual dining

A dim sum weekend brunch is one of those events that most often excludes vegetarians—pork and seafood are hidden where you least expect them. Not so at Vegetarian Dim Sum House. For just a few bucks per plate (three or four dumplings per order), you can afford to eat like a king. Tasty steamed Vegetarian mock Roast Pork Buns are light and doughy. Rice Flour Rolls are available with a variety of fillings like Chinese kale. Not everything on the menu is a winner. The Vegetarian Mock Shrimp Dumplings are devoid of flavor. You're best off skipping the entrées altogether—the Mock Pork with Spicy Cashew Nuts and Vegetables sounds a lot better than it tastes. For meatless main dishes, venture over to sister restaurant House of Vegetarian on Mott Street. And though the Dim Sum House is clean and comfortable compared to most Chinatown joints, don't expect much ambiance. Dim sum $2.25 per order, main dishes from $4 to $12.

VEGAN

★★ / $$

155. Vegetarian House

139 East 45th Street
(between Lexington and Third Avenues), 2nd floor
New York, NY 10017
212.490.0468

CHINESE

Hours:	Mon-Fri 11:30 a.m. to 10:00 p.m.
Payment:	Credit cards
Alcohol:	No
Atmosphere:	Casual dining

A great lunch hour alternative to generic midtown delis and pizza parlors, Vegetarian House is a bit hidden on the second floor, located above a take-out Chinese joint that you'd never give a second look. Unlike most Chinatown dives, the decor here is classy and comfortable. Don't be thrown off by the menu listings for beef, chicken, and seafood—everything is vegetarian. The chefs seem to have an extraordinary talent for preparing mock meat dishes. The protein chunks in Sesame Flavor Chicken look, feel, and taste more like chicken than anything you're likely to have tried before. Shrimp with Cashew Nuts is deceptive as well. Where they unfortunately go wrong is the abundance of onions and peppers in most dishes. The good news is that more than a hundred meatless dishes are offered, so you can experiment. Just don't miss out on the bargain lunch specials. Main dishes from $6 to $10.

VEGETARIAN WITH VEGAN CHOICES

★★★ / $$

156. Vegetarian's Paradise 2

144 West 4th Street
(between Macdougal Street and Sixth Avenue)
New York, NY 10012
212.260.7130; www.vp2-nyc.com

MULTIETHNIC

Hours:	Sun-Thu noon to 11:00 p.m.
	Fri-Sat noon to midnight
Payment:	Credit cards
Alcohol:	No
Atmosphere:	Casual dining

Vegetarian's Paradise 2 (completely unrelated to Vegetarian Paradise 3) may look like a suburban Chinese restaurant with green faux-marble accents throughout, but that's where the bad news ends. Due to its prime NYU-area location, it's crowded at night, but the wait for a table is never too long. Everything on the menu is fun and creative, with offerings from seemingly standard Chinese fare to meatless American classics. No, the Maryland Crab Cake doesn't taste anything like a real crab cake, but it's drizzled with an enjoyable Vidalia onion vinaigrette and served with tater tots. Harkow dumplings are as good as anything you can get in Chinatown. Golden Nuggets, crunchy soy chicken chunks with a tangy BBQ sauce, are a treat as well. All of the aforementioned dishes happen to be appetizers, which isn't a bad way to order. Order an assortment and share with friends. Main dishes from $9 to $11.

VEGAN

★★★ / $$

157. Viang Ping

210 East 23rd Street
(between Second and Third Avenues)
New York, NY 10010
212.481.8616

THAI

Hours:	Mon-Fri 11:00 a.m. to 11:00 p.m.
	Sat-Sun 2:00 p.m. to 11:00 p.m.
Payment:	Credit cards
Alcohol:	Beer
Atmosphere:	Casual dining

SVA students must be keeping this Thai gem a secret. It's understandable why—the menu features nearly forty vegetarian dishes for reasonable prices. Bamboo and Christmas lights adorn the walls for a slightly kitschy feel and the waitservice is personal and considerate, but you won't be thinking much about anything else once you try the food. Unlike most Thai restaurants that simply offer you a choice of tofu instead of meat, Viang Ping offers meatless house specialties, namely vegetarian duck. Both the texture and the smoky flavor are great, so try the spicy Pad Gra Prow with basil, onion, pepper, and chili sauce. Tao Hoo Tord, fried tofu with a sweet tamarind sauce, is a great way to start off the meal. All the standard Thai curry and noodle dishes are offered as well. If you've been disappointed by vegetarian Pad Thai elsewhere, then give it a try here and you're in for a treat. Main dishes from $7 to $9.

**FULL MENU WITH AMPLE VEGETARIAN
AND VEGAN CHOICES**

★★ / $$

158. Village Natural

46 Greenwich Avenue
(between Sixth and Seventh Avenues)
New York, NY 10011
212.727.0968

MULTIETHNIC

Hours:	Mon-Fri 11:00 a.m. to 11:00 p.m.
	Sat 10:00 a.m. to 11:00 p.m.
	Sun 10:00 a.m. to 10:00 p.m.
Payment:	Credit cards
Alcohol:	Wine and beer
Atmosphere:	Casual dining

If you and your veggie friends can't decide between Mexican, Asian, American, or Italian for dinner, you might want to head over to Village Natural. The menu is all over the map. There's nothing fussy about the decor—exposed brick walls and lots of wood—not to mention the food. Try a Veggie Cutlet Sandwich served with a side of corn chips, Broccoli and Tofu with your choice of Black Bean Sauce or Peanut Sauce, or the comforting Wheat Balls served over a big plate of artichoke spaghetti with tomato sauce. All of the entrées are amply sized, so you can skip the greasy Spring Roll appetizer. Dinner entrées are reasonably priced, but the lunch specials are dirt cheap, a nice plus for nearby NYU and New School students on a budget. Non-dairy shakes and fresh-squeezed juices are available, as well as herbal teas and natural sodas. Main dishes from $7 to $13.

**VEGETARIAN WITH VEGAN AND
SEAFOOD OFFERINGS**

★★ / $$$

159. Vittorio

308 Bleecker
(between Grove Street and Seventh Avenue South)
New York, NY 10014
212.463.0730; www.vittoriocri.com

ITALIAN

Hours:	Mon-Sat 5:30 p.m. to 11:00 p.m.
	Sun 2:00 p.m. to 10:00 p.m.
Payment:	Credit cards
Alcohol:	Full bar
Atmosphere:	Casual dining

Step into this trattoria-style restaurant in the West Village and you feel like you could be anywhere other than New York. Waiters laden with towering black pepper mills offer you freshly grated parmesan cheese with every dish. It's a bit of a cliché, and that's part of Vittorio's old-school charm. An entire page of the enormous menu is devoted to strictly vegetarian choices. As you'd expect, there are also plenty of antipasti offerings to choose from, such as roasted peppers stuffed with eggplant and sautéed broccoli rabe. Entrées include pastas and risotti. If you're looking for hearty, satisfying fare, it's hard to go wrong, but the Fettucine with Sautéed Artichoke Hearts is oversalted and the pasta texture is a bit soft. Risi & Fagilio features cannelini beans mixed with risotto—very filling but nothing spectacular. The highlight of the meal may be the complimentary hot breads. Main dishes from $10 to $15.

FULL MENU WITH VEGETARIAN AND VEGAN CHOICES

★★ / $

160. Viva Herbal Pizzeria

179 Second Avenue
(between East 11th and East 12th Streets)
New York, NY 10003
212.420.8801

ITALIAN, PIZZERIA

Hours:	Sun-Thu 11:30 a.m. to midnight
	Fri-Sat 11:30 a.m. to 12:30 a.m.
Payment:	Cash only
Alcohol:	No
Atmosphere:	Counter service with casual seating

New York City has more than its fair share of great pizza places, all of which serve at least a few meatless pies. So why all the fuss about a vegetarian pizza joint? Well for one, Viva Herbal is kosher. Plus, though it may be just psychological, it's nice to know that there's no pepperoni or sausage on the premises. In addition to traditional crust pies like the fragrant and fresh-tasting Al Pesto Pizza, you can try slices made with whole-wheat crusts, cornmeal crusts, and even spelt. There are vegan pies like the zesty, cheeseless Siciliana and ones with soy cheese such as the Il Fiore. Almost no dietary restriction goes unanswered. Check the menu for even more options: ravioli, baked ziti, veggie lasagna, calzones, and sautéed pasta dishes like a vegan Penne a la Vodka (available for dinner only). Pizza by the slice from $2 to $4 and main dishes and whole pizzas from $5 to $21.

KOSHER VEGETARIAN WITH VEGAN CHOICES

★★ / $

161. Viva Natural Pizzeria
(aka Cafe Viva)

64 East 34th Street
(between Madison and Park Avenues)
New York, NY 10016
212.779.4350

ITALIAN, PIZZERIA

Hours:	Sun-Thu 11:00 a.m. to 11:00 p.m.
	Fri 11:00 a.m. to 3:00 p.m.
	Sat 6:30 p.m. to 1:00 a.m.
Payment:	Credit cards
Alcohol:	No
Atmosphere:	Counter service with casual seating

Other locations:
  1802 Avenue M (at East 18th Street), Brooklyn, NY 11230,
    718.787.0050;
  Cafe Viva, 2578 Broadway (between 97th and 98th
    Streets), New York, NY 10025, 212.663.8482

Viva Natural looks just like any other pizzeria in Manhattan, right down to the Pepperoni Pies. Of course, that's soy pepperoni. Rest assured that everything here is vegetarian. There are wheat-free, spelt-crust pizzas like the Zen, with basil pesto and green-tea-herbed miso-tofu topping; it might seem a bit pricey, even by New York standards, but the serving size is huge, and you won't go hungry. Vegan pies are offered, served on whole-wheat crusts, like the Tutta Verde and the Vegeteriana. The aforementioned Soy Pepperoni Pizza is particularly enjoyable, especially for newbie vegetarians looking to satisfy a craving. A variety of vegetarian and vegan calzones, strombolis, and pasta dishes rounds out the menu. Viva Natural, located just a block from the Empire State Building, may not be much to look at, but the big crowds at lunch hour don't seem to mind a bit. Pizza slices from $2 to $4 and main dishes and whole pizzas from $5 to $23.

KOSHER VEGETARIAN WITH VEGAN CHOICES

★★★ / \$\$

162. Vynl

754 Ninth Avenue
(between West 50th and 51st Streets)
New York, NY 10019
212.974.2003

MULTIETHNIC

Hours:	Mon-Tue 11:00 a.m. to 11:00 p.m.
	Wed-Fri 11:00 a.m. to midnight
	Sat 9:30 a.m. to midnight
	Sun 9:30 a.m. to 11:00 p.m.
Payment:	Credit cards
Alcohol:	Full bar
Atmosphere:	Hip, casual dining

One of the coolest, yet laid-back restaurants in Hell's Kitchen, Vynl is almost always filled to capacity. You'll understand why once you've tried the food. The menus are presented inside old LP record sleeves; there's no shortage of reasonably priced vegetarian dishes here, clearly marked with V's for easy spotting. Even better, many of the Asian-style dishes are available with your choice of protein, including tofu of course. Start off with the crispy Butternut Squash Wontons with lemon-flavored soy sauce. If the Bar-B-Que Tofu Wrap sounds like something you've tried, think again—it's stuffed with bell peppers and flavored just right. The Red Curry with Tofu is as good as, if not better than, you can get at any Thai restaurant in Manhattan. Expect an upbeat crowd and a lot of noise here. Not the best place for intimate conversation, but you'll be too busy enjoying your food to mind. Main dishes from \$10 to \$12.

**FULL MENU WITH VEGETARIAN
AND VEGAN CHOICES**

★★ / \$\$

163. Wai Cafe

583 Sixth Avenue
(between West 15th and West 16th Streets)
New York, NY 10011
212.414.2003

MULTIETHNIC

Hours:	Open 24 hours
Payment:	Credit cards
Alcohol:	Wine and beer
Atmosphere:	Casual dining

Other locations:
201 First Avenue (between East 12th and East 13th Streets), New York, NY 10003, 212.388.1997

Wai Cafe's owners are apparently expecting big things—the second location on Sixth Avenue is massive. Whether or not they can start filling the restaurant remains to be seen, but the annoying music and slow kitchen service isn't going to help. With no beef or pork on the menu, there's plenty of room left for vegetarian offerings. It's a step in the right direction, but the chef stumbles when it comes to any preparation more complex than a salad. As the menu says, this is "lean cuisine," but that's no excuse for ordinary food. Pasta and noodle dishes are all over the map, which in this case means that they can't get anything quite right. Wai Fettucini is filling but dull, and you can get a better Pad Thai in just about any Thai restaurant in the city. Still, prices are reasonable and portions are ample. If you must dine here, try any of the veggie salads with the tasty carrot dressing. Main dishes from $7 to $10.

FULL MENU WITH VEGETARIAN AND VEGAN CHOICES

★ / $

164. Whole Earth Bakery & Kitchen

130 St. Mark's Place
(between First Avenue and Avenue A)
New York, NY 10009
212.677.7597; www.wholeearthbakery.com

AMERICAN, BAKERY

Hours:	Sun-Thu 9:00 a.m. to midnight
	Fri-Sat 9:00 a.m. to 11:00 p.m.
Payment:	Cash only
Alcohol:	No
Atmosphere:	Take-out counter with limited seating

Located within a stone's throw of Thompkins Square Park on St. Mark's Place, Whole Earth has no menus. Check the board on the wall for daily offerings, and plan to take your food with you to the park. There are a few seats available, but nothing about the decor is very inviting. Baked goods behind the counter are tempting, and vegans are sure to enjoy a slice of the dense and sweet Blueberry Cheesecake. Unfortunately, the savory options are less than, well, savory. Tofu and tempeh sandwiches sit wrapped in plastic for untold hours, so it should come as no surprise that they taste dry and bland by the time you get your hands on one. Cold, raw soups are a bit of an acquired taste and not very appealing even on a hot day. Without a doubt, the food here is good for you, but if taste is what you're looking for, you may be disappointed. Stick with the desserts. Main dishes from $4 to $8.

KOSHER VEGAN

★★★ / $
165. Whole Foods Market

> 250 Seventh Avenue (at West 24th Street)
> New York, NY 10001
> 212.294.5969; www.wholefoods.com

AMERICAN, MULTIETHNIC

Hours:	Daily 8:00 a.m. to 10:00 p.m.
Payment:	Credit cards
Alcohol:	No
Atmosphere:	Take-out service only

Other locations:

10 Columbus Circle (near East 59th Street and Broadway),New York, NY 10019, 212.823.9600;

4 Union Square South (between Broadway and University Place), New York, NY 10003, 212.673.5388;

220 3rd Street, Brooklyn, NY;

Greenwich St & Warren St, New York, NY;

Bowery & Houston St.,New York, NY

Now with about 150 stores, Whole Foods is growing fast, yet remains a bit of a novelty to most New Yorkers. It's one of the largest and cleanest markets in the city, offering a quality of produce and selection of natural food products few others can match. As if that's not impressive enough, they sell a vast array of prepared foods, including hot and cold serve-yourself salad bars, hot soups, and countless entrées from behind pristine glass cases at the rear of the store. If you can't decide what you're in the mood for, just fill up your tray with a bit of this and a scoop of that and pay by the pound. Prices are very reasonable, and the quality and bold flavors are even more impressive. You'll be hard-pressed to find something that isn't tasty. Signs alongside the trays list all of the ingredients, great if you have food allergies, but don't be surprised if the dishes are mislabeled. Hot and cold buffet sold by weight.

**FULL MENU WITH AMPLE VEGETARIAN
AND VEGAN CHOICES**

★★ / $$

166. Why Curry?

> 126 St. Mark's Place
> (between First Avenue and Avenue A)
> New York, NY 10009
> 212.473.1620
>
> THAI
>
> | | |
> |---|---|
> | Hours: | Sun-Thu 11:30 a.m. to 11:00 p.m. |
> | | Fri-Sat 11:30 a.m. to 11:30 p.m. |
> | Payment: | Credit cards |
> | Alcohol: | Wine and beer |
> | Atmosphere: | Casual dining |

Why Curry?'s prime location on busy St. Mark's, just a few doors away from Tompkins Square Park, has helped it survive in a city that's overrun with Thai restaurants. It's the kind of place where you feel right at home, cozy yet comfortable and totally casual, with lots of dark wood and exposed brick. So what makes Why Curry? different from countless other Thai joints? For one thing, nearly every dish on the menu—curries, rice dishes, sautéed dishes, and noodles—is available with a choice of protein, including tofu. As the restaurant name implies, curries are the star here, from spicy red and green to peanuty Massaman. Not that the Pad Thai is a slouch, but you can definitely do better, and you should skip the dumplings, just to be on the safe side. Main dishes from $7 to $8.

FULL MENU WITH AMPLE VEGETARIAN AND VEGAN OFFERINGS

★★★ / $$

167. Wild Ginger

> 380 Broome Street
> (between Mott and Mulberry Streets)
> New York, NY 10013
> 212.966.1883/2669; www.wildgingernyc.com
>
> PAN-ASIAN
>
> | | |
> |---|---|
> | Hours: | Mon-Thu 11:30 a.m. to 10:30 p.m. |
> | | Fri-Sat 11:30 a.m. to 11:00 p.m. |
> | | Sun 1:00 p.m. to 10:30 p.m. |
> | Payment: | Credit cards |
> | Alcohol: | No |
> | Atmosphere: | Casual dining |

Though the pan-Asian category of restaurants is overcrowded, Wild Ginger manages to stand out from the pack. The only complaint is that the cozy restaurant has already built up a loyal following and can be packed to capacity during peak hours; the charming waitstaff will get you seated quickly enough. At some similarly-themed restaurants, meat analogues like soy protein and seitan can sometimes be off-putting, but they're so well prepared here, you might even consider inviting some of your carnivore friends along to show them what they're missing. Appetizers such as pan-fried dumplings, Yam & Taro Tempura, and especially the Crispy Watercress & Soy Cheese Wontons are the perfect way to start the meal. All of the entrees are good, but a few dishes, like the Sweet & Sour Sesame Soy Protein, are sure to impress. Entrees from $10 to $13.

VEGETARIAN WITH MOSTLY VEGAN CHOICES

★★★ / $

168. Yonah Schimmel Knish Bakery

137 East Houston Street
(between Houston and Stanton)
New York, NY 10022
212.477.2858; www.yonahschimmel.com

JEWISH BAKERY

Hours:	Daily 9:00 a.m. to 7:00 p.m.
Payment:	Cash only
Alcohol:	No
Atmosphere:	Counter service with casual seating

Any respectable Jewish deli in the Big Apple serves knishes, but you've never really tried a knish until you've been to Yonah Schimmel. Everything is baked right on the premises, and with the almost constant crowds, turnover is very high. A little mustard is always nice, but these knishes are so fresh—flaky tender on the outside and moist on the inside—you can eat them plain. Fortunately, you get one free with any order for a dozen, so you can buy an assortment and snack on the way home. Varieties include broccoli, spinach, kasha, sweet potato, and more, as well as dessert flavors like apple strudel and blueberry-cheese. The value for your dollar is unbeatable for such a satisfying meal. Don't forget to order a Cherry-Lime Rickey before you're done. Knishes from $2 to $3.

KOSHER, MOSTLY VEGETARIAN CHOICES

★★ / $$

169. Yummy House

76 Third Avenue
(between East 11th and East 12th Streets)
New York, NY 10003
212.505.1668

CHINESE

Hours:	Sun-Thu 11:30 a.m. to 11:30 p.m.
	Fri-Sat 11:30 a.m. to midnight
Payment:	Credit cards
Alcohol:	No
Atmosphere:	Casual dining

Whether it's the speedy service, reasonable prices, or the prime location near NYU and New School dorms, Yummy House must be onto something because they pack in the crowds during peak hours. While it may lack the ambiance of trendy restaurants around Union Square, it's cleaner and more comfortable than your average Chinese take-out joint, so dining in is definitely an option. There are plenty of meatless choices on the menu, just not too many winners. Steamed Vegetable Dumplings are bland and doughy. Many of the amply portioned fried tofu dishes, though tasty, are slightly sweet. General Tso's tastes more like a sweet-and-sour dish. Sesame Tofu is sugary and cloying as well. If you live or work in the neighborhood, Yummy House is a solid contender for fast-food Chinese; otherwise it's not worth going out of your way for. Main dishes from $6 to $8.

**FULL MENU WITH VEGETARIAN
AND VEGAN CHOICES**

★★ / $$

170. Zenith

311 West 48th Street
(between Eighth and Ninth Avenues)
New York, NY 10036
212.262.8080

PAN-ASIAN

Hours:	Daily 11:30 a.m. to 10:00 p.m.
Payment:	Credit cards
Alcohol:	Full bar
Atmosphere:	Casual dining

Don't be surprised if the waiter hands you a sushi menu, because this is, literally, two restaurants in one. Badly in need of a makeover, Zenith attracts a lot of tourists and the pretheater crowd due to its location just off Times Square in Hell's Kitchen. The menu (once you get the right one) is exhaustive. With evocative names like Enchanting Bug, Succulent Paradise, and Purple Moon, the detailed dish descriptions and photographs come in handy. Don't be deceived by the "pasta specials"; everything here tastes like Asian food. There are a few gems like the Green Pyramid with shredded black mushrooms, and the portions are huge, but like many Asian vegetarian restaurants, the food is a bit heavy and greasy. Health-conscious vegetarians may want to steer clear. And with the ever-popular Zen Palate located just a few blocks away, Zenith is up against some pretty stiff competition. Main dishes $13 to $15.

VEGETARIAN WITH VEGAN CHOICES
AND SEPARATE FISH MENU

★★★ / $$

171. Zen Palate

34 Union Square East
(at East 16th Street)
New York, NY 10003
212.614.9291

PAN-ASIAN

Hours:	*Mon-Sat 11:30 a.m. to 11:00 p.m.*
	Sun noon to 10:30 p.m.
Payment:	*Credit cards*
Alcohol:	*No*
Atmosphere:	*Stylish, casual dining, take-out*
	counter, and upscale dining upstairs

Other locations:
663 Ninth Avenue (at West 46th Street), New York, NY 10036, 212.582.1669;
2170 Broadway (between West 76th and West 77th Streets), New York, NY 10024, 212.501.7768

With three locations and counting, trendy Zen Palate draws a capacity crowd at all hours. Two restaurants in one, there's a dining room upstairs with a more upscale menu, nice for a special occasion or a business meeting, while the more affordable menu downstairs lends itself to hip and casual dining with friends or people-watching from the sidewalk seating. Zen Palate's heavy faux-meat menu isn't going to win over any carnivores, but devout veggies have come to know and love dishes like Sweet & Sour Sensation or the wheat-gluten-based Sesame Medallions. Entrées are served with tasty spring rolls and brown rice—a complete meal for a great price. On the other hand, a dinner for two with drinks in the quieter, elegant dining room could run you fifty dollars or more, so don't forget the credit card. Café-area main dishes $7 to $8. Restaurant-area main dishes $14 to $16.

VEGETARIAN WITH VEGAN CHOICES

Brooklyn

★★★ / $$

1. Bliss Café

191 Bedford Avenue
(between North 6th and North 7th Streets)
Williamsburg, Brooklyn, NY 11211
718.599.2574

AMERICAN

Hours:	Mon-Fri 9:00 a.m. to 11:00 p.m.
	Sat-Sun 10:00 a.m. to 11:00 p.m.
Payment:	Cash only
Alcohol:	No
Atmosphere:	Hip, casual dining

Just steps away from the L-train's Bedford Avenue station, the charming Bliss Café is appropriately named. Plants hang in the window, the decor is both casual and hip, and the walls feature work by local artists. Best of all, this is the kind of place where patrons know the friendly staff by name. Of course that kind of loyalty means that it can be tough to get a table. Fortunately, it's worth the wait. The brunch menu features fruity pancakes, tofu scramble, tempeh bacon, and more. With plenty of vegan offerings, the menu dispels any confusion with complete ingredient listings alongside each dish. Soups change daily and can be very satisfying. Sandwiches like the Grilled Tempeh or the Marinated Tofu are piled high, a terrific value for your money. If you order too much and can't finish your meal, don't say no one warned you. Main dishes $8 to $10.

VEGETARIAN WITH VEGAN CHOICES

★★ / $$$

2. Blue/Green Organic Juice Cafe

25 Jay Street (between John and Plymouth Streets)
Dumbo, Brooklyn, NY 11201
718.722.7541; www.bluegreenjuice.com

MULTIETHNIC

Hours:	9:00 a.m. to 6:00 p.m.
Payment:	Cash
Alcohol:	No
Atmosphere:	Take-out service with ample seating

Other locations:
248 Mott Street, New York, NY;
203 East 74th Street, New York, NY;
Take-out service with casual seating

Venture out to the Dumbo area of Brooklyn to check out The Plant, a massive 4,000 square foot natural living, wellness, and educational facility, which should be up and running by the time you read this. The menu at Blue/Green is totally vegan and raw, and much of it sounds tempting, but like all raw food, nothing is what you'd expect. If they say "noodles," then you can count on some julienned veggies that resemble noodles. The menu is perfect for anyone following a very restricted, healthful diet, but the problem is that lunch for two people might cost as much as forty dollars, and you're likely to still be hungry afterwards. The desserts on the other hand are outstanding, and you can't help but wonder how they make these treats taste so good with only raw ingredients. Best of all, the counter staff will practically insist that you taste test the goodies before you make a choice. Main dishes from $12 to $20.

RAW, VEGAN

★★ / $
3. Cafe Kai

151 Smith Street
(between Bergen and Wyckoff Streets)
Boerum Hill, Brooklyn, NY 11021
718.596.3466

MULTIETHNIC

Hours:	Mon–Fri 8:00 a.m. to 7:00 p.m.
	Sat 10:30 a.m. to 7:30 p.m.
	Sun 11:00 a.m. to 5:00 p.m.
Payment:	Cash only
Alcohol:	No
Atmosphere:	Take-out service with casual seating

Near the north end of Brooklyn's Smith Street restaurant strip, Cafe Kai is easy to overlook as just another coffee shop or juice joint. You wouldn't be entirely wrong; there are terrific vegetable and fruit juices, not to mention tasty smoothies and shakes like the Tropical Paradise made with mango, coconut milk, pineapple, and banana. Once you stop in, you'll find the only completely vegetarian menu in the neighborhood, and a creative one at that. Dirt-cheap turnovers (patties) are a treat; the crusts are flaky with your choice of fillings like tofu, "mock duck," or "mock fish." Sandwiches like the Avocado-Tofu Wrap are equally enjoyable. Seating is limited but casual and cozy—it's a great place to read the newspaper while you enjoy the daily soup special such as Butternut Squash Bisque. Tasty vegan desserts and muffins are available as well. Main dishes from $4 to $8.

VEGETARIAN WITH VEGAN CHOICES

★★ / $

4. Caribbean Delicacy Restaurant

575 Lincoln Place
(between Bedford and Franklin Avenues)
Crown Heights, Brooklyn, NY 11216
718.778.7558

CARIBBEAN

Hours:	Daily 8:00 a.m. to 9:00 p.m.
Payment:	Cash only
Alcohol:	No
Atmosphere:	Take-out service only

A convenient location just around the block from the Franklin Avenue subway station and seriously spicy fare make Caribbean Delicacy worth a trip to Crown Heights. Just check a map before you start wandering around the neighborhood. Don't be scared off by the bulletproof glass and the lack of seating, but if you're not a chile fiend, then you may want to stay clear. As the friendly owners will tell you, the menu varies daily, and they'll be happy to explain each and every dish. On the occasion of this review, it was "curry day." Order a small combo platter, and take a walk over to one of the benches on tree-lined Eastern Parkway to enjoy your food. Just don't forget to ask for a refreshing sorrel juice, or two, to cool down the spicy heat. The fresh lemonade is a great choice too, but it sells out as fast as they can make a batch. Combo plates from $6 to $10.

VEGAN

★★ / $

5. "D" Ital Shak

989 Nostrand Avenue
(between Empire Boulevard and Sullivan Place)
Flatbush, Brooklyn, NY 11225
718.756.6557

CARIBBEAN

Hours:	Open 24 hours
Payment:	Cash only
Alcohol:	No
Atmosphere:	Counter service with very limited seating

Other locations:
  305 Halsey Street (at Throop Avenue), Crown Heights, Brooklyn, NY 11216, 718.573.3752

Though it's conveniently located just steps from the Sterling Avenue subway station, you don't want to spend too much time in East Flatbush unless you really know your way around the area; there is a reason why the cash register at "D" Ital Shak is positioned behind bulletproof glass. As with most Brooklyn Caribbean restaurants, seating is almost nonexistent. Menu choices vary day to day, so your best bet is to ask for a bargain combination platter and sample a little bit of everything. Big slabs of sweet-and-sour tofu, curried soy chunks, and home-style black-eyed peas are all mild flavored but satisfying. Order the tender and salty soy fish while you're at it, and you won't be disappointed. For a complete experience, ask for fresh grapefruit juice and a slice of the impressively moist whole-wheat pineapple cake. Combo plates from $6 to $10.

VEGAN

★★ / $

6. Famous Pita

935 Coney Island Avenue
(between Ditmas and Webster Avenues)
Midwood, Brooklyn, NY 11230
718.284.0161

MIDDLE EASTERN

Hours:	Sun-Thu 11:00 a.m. to midnight
	Fri 11:00 a.m. to 4:00 p.m.
	Closed Sat
Payment:	Credit cards
Alcohol:	No
Atmosphere:	Counter service with casual seating

It's a little bit of a trip on the Q train to get to Famous Pita, well worthwhile for falafel fanatics if for no other reason than to see the automatic falafel-making machine drop the balls into hot oil for deep frying. Otherwise, this is an entirely do-it-yourself experience. The counter staff hands you a puffy pita bread or lafah bread (both good choices, baked fresh on the premises), and the rest is up to you. Add as many falafel balls as you'd like, then top your sandwich with a variety of slaws, relishes, pickles, sauces, and more. If you opt for the oversized and slightly chewy lafah bread, you can expect to make a mess. Seating is very casual, if a bit dingy, so don't plan on staying for long. Famous Pita may not be up to the level of nearby Olympic Pita, but it comes pretty close. Sandwiches from $3 to $4.

**KOSHER MENU WITH VEGETARIAN
AND VEGAN CHOICES**

★★ / $

7. Foodswings

295 Grand Street
(between Roebling and Havemeyer Streets)
Williamsburg, Brooklyn, NY 11211
718.388.1919; www.foodswings.net

AMERICAN AND MULTIETHNIC

Hours:	Tue-Thu 5:00 p.m. to midnight
	Fri 5:00 p.m. to 2:00 a.m.
	Sat noon to 2:00 a.m.
	Sun 2:00 p.m. to 11:00 p.m.
Payment:	Cash
Alcohol:	No
Atmosphere:	Take-out service with casual seating

This trendy strip of Grand Street in Williamsburg is the perfect spot for a place like Foodswings, with it's hip, yet casual vibe. It's a local haunt, so you can expect it to be very busy on a Friday or Saturday night. Don't let the crowd worry you as you peruse the kitschy menu. Yes, you're reading right—they serve all vegan food in the form of chicken parmgiana, tuna salad, grilled cheese, rootbeer floats, and more than a dozen flavors of milkshakes. So if you're craving the food of your childhood, this is the right spot to be in. You might want to skip the veggie burgers though, since they aren't much different from what you can make yourself at home. The drumsticks, offered in a variety of flavors like BBQ or Buffalo Style, are favorites. Note that the menu choices are reduced to a special list of "munchies" after 11:00 p.m. on Friday and Saturday nights. Main dishes from $5 to $8.

VEGAN

★★ / $

8. Four Seasons

2281 Church Avenue
(between Bedford and Flatbush Avenues)
Flatbush, Brooklyn, NY 11226
718.693.7996

CARIBBEAN

Hours:	Mon-Fri 7:30 a.m. to 10:00 p.m.
	Sat-Sun 7:30 a.m. to midnight
Payment:	Cash only
Alcohol:	No
Atmosphere:	Counter service with casual seating

Four Seasons in Brooklyn's Flatbush neighborhood is about as far removed from its 4-star midtown namesake as you can possibly get: vegan food, a juice bar, dairy-free baked goods, loud reggae music, and no table service. Unlike most Brooklyn Caribbean joints, seating is ample, but unless you happen to be in the area, Four Seasons may not be worth the trip. You don't want to be strolling around on Church Avenue after dark, and the food isn't on par with nearby Veggie Castle, though the friendly staff is quick to offer taste samples if you're unsure about what to order. For dirt-cheap prices, they'll fill up a tray with an assortment of soy protein and tofu-based, Caribbean-style entrées and vegetable sides. This is home-style comfort food, but if you're looking for something bold and spicy, you've come to the wrong place. Combo platters from $6 to $10.

VEGAN

★★ / $$

9. The Greens

128 Montague Street (at Henry Street)
Brooklyn Heights, Brooklyn, NY 11201
718.246.0088

CHINESE

Hours:	Mon-Thu 11:00 a.m. to 10:30 p.m.
	Fri 11:00 a.m. to 11:00 p.m.
	Sat noon to 11:00 p.m.
	Sun 1:00 p.m. to 10:30 p.m.
Payment:	Credit cards
Alcohol:	No
Atmosphere:	Casual dining

Overlooking tree-lined Montague and Henry Streets in Brooklyn Heights' gorgeous historic district, The Greens offers an exhaustive selection of vegetarian Chinese food, more than making up for the abrupt waitservice. Skip the complimentary, mealy boiled peanuts, and avoid the disappointing dumplings. The amply sized entrées are the real treat here. Wheat gluten and soy protein are available in all forms: sliced, battered, fried, shredded, sautéed, and more. Some of the dishes are almost eerie; the Yin-Yang "mini mushroom steak" has a chewy and distinctively meat-like texture, covered in an addictive sesame sauce. Battered Soy Bean Gluten and Taro Root in House BBQ Sauce is enjoyable as well. Lunch specials (available on Saturdays as well) are a remarkable value, with more than thirty dishes to choose from. Main dishes from $6 to $13.

KOSHER VEGETARIAN WITH VEGAN CHOICES

★★★ / $

10. Imhotep's

> 734 Nostrand Avenue
> (between Park and Prospect Places)
> Crown Heights, Brooklyn, NY 11216
> 718.493.2395

CARIBBEAN

Hours:	Daily 9:00 a.m. to 9:00 p.m.
Payment:	Cash only
Alcohol:	No
Atmosphere:	Health food market with counter service and limited seating

Not too far from the Nostrand Avenue stop on the number 3 train, Imhotep's is one vegan Caribbean restaurant in Crown Heights that's undoubtedly worth the trip. Primarily a health food store, it's not apparent from the outside that Imhotep's serves prepared food at all. Consider yourself fortunate for having read this review. Like most Caribbean joints, the menu varies daily. Keep your fingers crossed that they'll be serving the tangy, spiced soy beef—not even Manhattan favorites like Red Bamboo or Vegetarian Paradise 3 can top this dish. Seven dollars buys you an oversized combination plate. The Vanilla Cake is another winner, one of those desserts that tastes way too good to be vegan. Unlike most restaurants in the area, there are a few tables available for dining in. It's nothing fancy, but it's comfortable. Combo plates from $6 to $10.

VEGAN

★★ / $

11. Irie Vegetarian Food

> 804 Nostrand Avenue
> (between Lincoln Place and Eastern Parkway)
> Crown Heights, Brooklyn, NY 11216
> 718.493.2451

CARIBBEAN

Hours:	Daily 8:00 a.m. to 8:00 p.m.
Payment:	Cash only
Alcohol:	No
Atmosphere:	Take-out service with very limited bar-stool seating

Like many take-out restaurants in Crown Heights, the counter help at Irie works behind bulletproof glass. In fact, nothing about the style of this restaurant is very inviting, but at least it's not far from the Nostrand

Avenue subway station. Seating is limited, so plan to take your food to Eastern Parkway and find yourself a park bench. There are no menus, so just order a combo plate and bring your appetite. Ask for a beet or sorrel juice and inquire about the daily soup offerings. Again, like other vegetarian restaurants in the area, you can expect a lot of nameless curried soy-chunk dishes, along with rice, veggies, pasta (lo mein), and more. Though satisfying, it's far from the best that the neighborhood has to offer; it's too tough to compete with Imhotep's, Caribbean Delicacy, and Ras Diggi, all of which are within walking distance. Combo plates from $6 to $10.

VEGAN

★★ / $$

12. Lemongrass Grill

> 61A Seventh Avenue
> (between Berkeley and Lincoln Places)
> Park Slope, Brooklyn, NY 11217
> 718.399.7100
>
> **THAI**
>
> | | |
> |---|---|
> | **Hours:** | Mon-Fri noon to 10:30 p.m. |
> | | Sat-Sun noon to 11:30 p.m. |
> | **Payment:** | Credit cards |
> | **Alcohol:** | Beer and wine |
> | **Atmosphere:** | Casual dining |

Other locations:

> 2534 Broadway (between West 94th and West 95th Streets), New York, NY 10025, 212.666.0888;
>
> 138 East 34th Street (between Lexington and Third Avenues), New York, NY 10016, 212.213.3317;
>
> 80 University Place (at East 11th Street), New York, NY 10003, 212.604.9870;
>
> 53 Avenue A (at East 4th Street), New York, NY 10009, 212.674.3538;
>
> 74-76 Seventh Avenue South (at Barrow Street), New York, NY 10014, 212.242.0606

See page 74 for details.

**FULL MENU WITH VEGETARIAN
AND VEGAN CHOICES**

★★★ / $$

13. Life Cafe

983 Flushing Avenue
Bushwick, Brooklyn, NY, 10026
718.386.1133; www.lifecafenyc.com

AMERICAN AND MULTIETHNIC

Hours:	Daily 10:00 a.m. to midnight
	(bar open until 4:00 a.m.)
Payment:	Credit cards
Alcohol:	Full bar
Atmosphere:	Casual dining

Other locations:

343 East 10th Street (at Avenue B), New York, NY 10009,
212.477.8791

See page 75 for details.

FULL MENU WITH VEGAN CHOICES

★★★ / $

14. Olympic Pita

1419 Coney Island Avenue (between Avenues J and K),
Midwood, Brooklyn, NY 11230; 718.258.6222

MIDDLE EASTERN

Hours:	Daily noon to 1:00 a.m.
Payment:	Credit cards
Alcohol:	No
Atmosphere:	Counter service with casual seating

Wherever you are and whatever you're doing, if you're
a falafel lover, then hop on the Q train and head out to
Olympic Pita now. Yes, it's that good. You won't find
any chewy, stale pitas here. Breads are baked right
behind the counter. Don't be surprised if your bread is
served piping hot, fresh from the oven. For vegetarians,
the only choice is whether you want a puffy pita bread
or the oversized lafah bread; either way, you can't go
wrong. The counter staff will make your falafel fresh to
order and stuff the balls into your sandwich, along
with some hummus. The rest is up to you—a salad bar
offers a choice of toppings, including slaws, pickles,
relishes, and sauces. Unlike nearby Famous Pita, the
seating here is clean and comfortable. Falafel doesn't
get any better than this. Sandwiches from $3 to $4.

KOSHER MENU WITH VEGETARIAN
AND VEGAN CHOICES

★★ / $

15. Original Vegetarian and Seafood Restaurant

752 Nostrand Avenue
(between Park and Sterling Places)
Crown Heights, Brooklyn, NY 11216
718.778.6660

CARIBBEAN

Hours:	Daily 8:00 a.m. to 9:00 p.m.
Payment:	Cash only
Alcohol:	No
Atmosphere:	Counter service with limited bar-stool seating

The name of this restaurant says it all—they opened more than twenty years ago, long before any of the other Crown Heights Caribbean vegan joints turned up. Before you hop on the number 2 or 5 train to Crown Heights, be forewarned that Nostrand Avenue isn't the kind of neighborhood where you want to be wandering around aimlessly. Bar-stool seating along the dark walls and loud Jamaican music sum up the ambiance, if you can call it that, not offering much refuge from the busy street. Like most Caribbean joints, $7 buys you a platter filled with a little bit of everything: soy beef chunks, simmered greens, pasta salad, and rice. Unlike anything you're likely to see elsewhere, the ground-beef-style TVP dish is one of the highlights. Even better is the bread-pudding-like cake—moist and sweet, it's one of those desserts that tastes almost too good to be vegan. Combo plates from $6 to $10.

VEGAN WITH SEAFOOD CHOICES

★★ / $

16. Ras Diggi Ital & Vegetable Corner Rastaurant

819 Park Place
(between Nostrand and Rogers Avenues)
Crown Heights, Brooklyn, NY 11216
718.604.8585

CARIBBEAN

Hours:	Mon-Fri 9:00 a.m. to 10:00 p.m.
	Fri-Sat 9:00 a.m. to midnight
	Closed Sun
Payment:	Cash only
Alcohol:	No
Atmosphere:	Take-out service only

"Rastaurant" isn't a misspelling. One visit to Ras Diggi and you'll understand; you're likely to be the only customer who isn't a Rastafarian. Located not too far from the number 4 train and just off busy Nostrand Avenue, you need to know your way around Crown Heights before venturing out this way. A daytime visit is recommended. Don't expect seating or any ambiance whatsoever. What you can expect is humble and satisfying Caribbean dishes with a kick. They cook three times a day and menu offerings change regularly, so consider yourself to be very fortunate if they're serving the dumpling soup—thick and hearty with slightly sweet dough balls, potato, and carrots. Lo mein noodles with beef soy chunks is enjoyable as well. Hot sauce is on the counter for extra spice. Just be sure to order a mango or sorrel juice to cool down your taste buds. Main dishes from $4 to $6.

VEGAN

★★ / $$

17. Red Hot

349 Seventh Avenue (at 10th Street)
Park Slope, Brooklyn, NY 11215
718.369.0700

CHINESE

Hours:	Mon-Thu 11:30 a.m. to 10:30 p.m.
	Fri-Sat 11:30 a.m. to 11:00 p.m.
	Sun 1:00 p.m. to 10:30 p.m.
Payment:	Credit cards
Alcohol:	Wine and beer
Atmosphere:	Casual dining

Why bother hopping on the subway and braving the crowds of Chinatown when you can get vegetarian Chinese this good right in Park Slope? And while most Chinatown restaurants are about as charming as a hole in the wall, Red Hot is entirely comfortable. A huge portion of the menu is devoted to meatless dishes, and though the signage bills this restaurant as Szechuan, even the dishes marked as "hot & spicy" are relatively mild. Be sure to start off with an order of Vegetable Dumplings, as good as you'll try on either side of the East River. If you're tired of ordering veggie dumplings that resemble the texture of Play-Doh, you're in for a very pleasant surprise. Sautéed Veggie Pork with BBQ Sauce is another winner. If you're not a big fan of wheat gluten, there are plenty of sautéed vegetable offerings, as well as vegetarian soups, and noodle and fried-rice dishes. Main dishes from $7 to $9.

**FULL MENU WITH VEGETARIAN
AND VEGAN CHOICES**

★★ / $
18. Rice

81 Washington Street (near Front Street)
Dumbo, Brooklyn, NY 11201
718.222.9880; www.riceny.com

MULTIETHNIC

Hours:	Daily noon to 10:00 p.m.
Payment:	Cash only
Alcohol:	Beer
Atmosphere:	Hip, casual dining

Other locations:

227 Mott Street (between Prince and Spring Streets), New York, NY 10012, 212.226.5775;

118 Lexington Avenue, New York, NY 10016, 212.686.5400;

166 DeKalb Avenue (at Cumberland Street), Fort Green, Brooklyn, NY 11217, 718.858.2700

See page 103 for details.

**FULL MENU WITH VEGETARIAN
AND VEGAN CHOICES**

★★★ / $$
19. Sea

114 North 6th Street
(between Berry and Wythe Streets)
Williamsburg, Brooklyn, NY 11211
718.834.8850; www.spicenyc.net

THAI

Hours:	Sun-Thu 11:30 a.m. to 1:00 a.m.
	Fri-Sat 11:30 a.m. to 2:00 a.m.
Payment:	Credit cards
Alcohol:	Full bar
Atmosphere:	Stylish, casual dining

Other locations:

75 Second Avenue (between East 4th and East 5th Streets),
New York, NY 10003, 212.228.5505

Despite the name, Sea has nothing to do with seafood;
it's an anagram for "South East Asian." Regarding the
decor of the Brooklyn location, no words do it justice.
Take a trip to Williamsburg on the L train to see for
yourself, and prepare to be amazed. Long waits for a
table are not uncommon, despite the vast size of the
restaurant, and you can expect a club-like vibe on the
weekends, including a live DJ, so stay away if you're
interested in quiet conversation. As if Thai-inspired cook-
ing and bargain prices weren't enticing enough, the
menu turns out to be very veggie friendly—nearly every
dish is offered with tofu and/or vegetables. Plate presen-
tation is stylish but not fussy, and most everything is
well prepared. Start off with Po-Pia Sod, vegetarian
rolls with peanut and tamarind dipping sauces. Malay
Massaman Curry is sweet and mildly spiced. Noodle
dishes are all tasty as well. Main dishes from $7 to $8.

**FULL MENU WITH AMPLE VEGETARIAN
AND VEGAN CHOICES**

★★ / $
20. Second Helpings

448 9th Street (at Seventh Avenue)
Park Slope, Brooklyn, NY 11215
718.965.1925

MULTIETHNIC

Hours:	Tue-Fri 11:00 a.m. to 8:30 p.m.
	Sat-Sun 10:30 a.m. to 8:00 p.m.
	Closed Mon
Payment:	Cash only
Alcohol:	No
Atmosphere:	Counter service with casual seating

Just steps away from the Seventh Avenue F train subway station, Second Helpings offers wholesome, organic meals for picking up on the way home after work. A majority of the customers must be regulars because the friendly staff greets everyone like a best friend just walked in the door. Don't bother with the menu—just gaze into the refrigerated cases and see what looks good. You'll find globe-trotting entrées such as Portobello Mushroom Lasagna or Sweet Potato and Roasted Corn Empanadas. Sides like Organic Squash Vermicelli and roasted root vegetables complete the meal. Although the selection is exhaustive and the vegan and wheat-free cookies are divine, the restaurant's only failing is that everything is prepared in advance. Your food can be reheated upon request, but nothing beats a fresh-cooked hot meal. Main dishes from $7 to $10.

FULL MENU WITH VEGETARIAN AND VEGAN CHOICES

★★★ / $

21. Siggy's

76 Henry Street
(between Pineapple and Orange Streets)
Brooklyn Heights, Brooklyn, NY 11201
718.237.3199

AMERICAN AND MULTIETHNIC

Hours:	8:00 a.m. to 10:00 p.m.
Payment:	Credit cards
Alcohol:	No
Atmosphere:	Casual dining

Conveniently located near the 2/3 train stop at Clark Street and practically in the shadow of the Brooklyn Bridge, Siggy's is definitely worth a trip across the river. Unfortunately, locals already know and love Siggy's, and it can be a bit of a wait for a table during peak hours. Once you've tried it, you'll understand what the fuss is all about. The menu sounds deceptively simple; you aren't prepared for just how good the food is going to be. Quinoa Spinach Cakes are so tasty, you might want to double your order. The Tofurkey Hickory sandwich is better than similar-sounding sandwiches served at any veggie restaurant in the entire Big Apple. You'll devour the Spinach Feta Ravioli. And the laid-back vibe makes you feel right at home. One unfair complaint: why isn't there a Siggy's in every neighborhood? Main dishes from $7 to $11.

FULL ORGANIC MENU WITH VEGETARIAN AND VEGAN CHOICES

★★ / $

22. Strictly Vegetarian

2268 Church Avenue
(between Bedford and Flatbush Avenues)
Flatbush, Brooklyn, NY 11226
718.284.2543

CARIBBEAN

Hours:	Mon–Thu 11:00 a.m. to 10:00 p.m.
	Fri–Sat 11:00 a.m. to midnight
	Closed Sun
Payment:	Cash only
Alcohol:	No
Atmosphere:	Counter service with limited
	bar-stool seating

It may be a short walk from the Church Avenue stop on the Q train to Strictly Vegetarian, but this isn't a neighborhood you want to be wandering around in alone, especially at night. However, if you like your meatless fare with a kick, don't let that scare you away from making a trip to Flatbush. Seriously spicy Caribbean curries are the big draw. Strictly Vegetarian's menu changes daily and none of the dishes are labeled—just ask the friendly staff to explain what's available. Better yet, choose a tray size and let them stuff it with a little of everything. Entrées feature lots of soy protein chunks and tofu, with veggies and rice to temper the heat. Pumpkin curry is a highlight, when it's available. Pass on the dairy-free, whole-wheat desserts, unless you like your cookies soft and squishy. Combo plates from $6 to $10.

VEGAN

★★ / $$

23. Tchefa

512 Flatbush Avenue
(between Lefferts Avenue and Empire Boulevard)
Flatbush, Brooklyn, NY 11225
718.284.8742

CARIBBEAN, AMERICAN

Hours:	Mon–Fri 4:00 p.m. to 9:00 p.m.
	Sat–Sun noon to 10:00 p.m.
Payment:	Credit cards
Alcohol:	No
Atmosphere:	Counter service with casual seating

Just steps from the Prospect Park subway station and not too far of a walk from the Brooklyn Botanic Gardens, Tchefa is a welcome change of pace because, unlike most Crown Heights and Flatbush vegetarian restaurants, you can actually sit down and enjoy your food at this one. Tchefa is both clean and comfortable, with friendly service too. Signs in the window call Tchefa a sandwich bar, although there were no sandwiches in sight on the occasion of this review. Tasty curried veggie patties are as close as you can get to handheld food. You won't find any menus either, so just point to whatever looks tempting, namely the Southern-style cornmeal-crusted BBQ "shrimp" and jerk "chicken." Side dishes are lackluster by comparison, especially the macaroni and cheese. But portion sizes are huge—the large combination plate is large enough to feed two people. Combo plates from $6 to $10.

VEGETARIAN WITH MOSTLY VEGAN CHOICES

★★ / $$
24. Thai Sesame

160 Smith Street
(between Bergen and Wyckoff Streets),
Boerum Hill, Brooklyn, NY 11201
718.935.0101

THAI

Hours:	Daily 11:00 a.m. to 3:00 p.m.,
	5:00 p.m. to 11:00 p.m.
Payment:	Credit cards
Alcohol:	Beer and wine
Atmosphere:	Casual dining

Not far from Boerum Hill–favorite Tuk Tuk, Thai Sesame is up against some tough competition, though it deserves a nod for its intimate atmosphere: soft pink walls, rustic tiled floors, dark wood banquettes, and soothing music. The extensive menu holds its own as well; a majority of dishes are available with your choice of protein, including tofu, making Thai Sesame seriously veggie friendly. Just watch out for unlisted fish sauce in dishes like Som Tum, a sweet and spicy papaya salad. Chile-fanatics will love the vegetable-packed curries. Even if you specify that you'd like your Yellow Curry mild, make sure that you have plenty of water on hand. Pad See Ew, sautéed flat rice noodles with eggs and Chinese broccoli, is slightly sweet and a great choice to balance out the spicier dishes. Main dishes from $6 to $8.

**FULL MENU WITH VEGETARIAN
AND VEGAN CHOICES**

★★ / $$

25. Tofu on 7th

226 Seventh Avenue
(between 3rd and 4th Streets)
Park Slope, Brooklyn, NY 11215
718.768.5273

CHINESE

Hours:	Mon-Thu 11:30 a.m. to 10:30 p.m.
	Fri-Sat 11:30 a.m. to 11:00 p.m.
	Sun 1:00 p.m. to 10:30 p.m.
Payment:	Credit cards
Alcohol:	No
Atmosphere:	Casual dining

A taste of suburbia on tree-lined Seventh Avenue in Park Slope: impersonal waitstaff, mirrored walls, and marbleized Formica, not to mention the sound of clanking pots and pans echoing from the kitchen, are some of the things you have to look forward to at Tofu on 7th. Table service is offered, but if you live in the neighborhood, plan on ordering takeout, or even better, call for delivery. Before you Manhattanites run for the subway, it's fair to point out that the name is a bit misleading; Tofu on 7th offers plenty of chicken, beef, pork, and seafood, but with sixty meatless dishes, vegetarians certainly won't go hungry. When compared with Chinatown offerings, the food quality leaves something to be desired. General Tso's "Chicken" is served with a tangy, citrusy sauce, but is a bit chewy. House Buddah Delight is for tofu lovers only. This is reliable takeout for locals. Main dishes from $7 to $10.

**FULL MENU WITH AMPLE VEGETARIAN
AND VEGAN CHOICES**

★★★ / $$

26. Tuk Tuk

204 Smith Street
(between Baltic and Butler Streets)
Boerum Hill, Brooklyn, NY 11201
718.222.5598

THAI

Hours:	Sun-Thu noon to 10:15 p.m.
	Fri-Sat noon to 11:15 p.m.
Payment:	Cash only
Alcohol:	Beer and wine
Atmosphere:	Stylish, casual dining

Transplant this stylish restaurant to the streets of Soho and it would fit right in. Fortunately for Brooklyn hipsters, Tuk Tuk is conveniently located on the Smith Street restaurant strip. Try to grab one of the tables with a couch and get ready for food that is spicy, salty, sour, and sweet, just the way good Thai food should be. Noodle dishes are one of the many highlights of the menu, including standards such as Pad Thai and the spicier Pad Kee-Mao with chili paste, garlic, and basil, most of which are available in meatless versions. Curries, though fiery, are equally good and, as the kind staff will explain, can be adjusted to suit your personal taste. All available without meat, red, green and Massaman curries are offered, as well as a few more unique ones such as the Jungle Curry prepared with chili paste, eggplant, mushrooms, basil, string beans, and bamboo shoots. Main dishes from $7 to $9.

FULL MENU WITH VEGETARIAN AND VEGAN CHOICES

★★ / $

27. Uncle Moe's Burrito and Taco Shop

341 Seventh Avenue
(between 9th and 10th Streets)
Park Slope, Brooklyn, 11215
718.965.0006

MEXICAN

Hours:	Daily noon to 10:00 p.m.
Payment:	Credit cards
Alcohol:	No
Atmosphere:	Counter service with casual seating

Other locations:

14 West 19th Street (between Fifth and Sixth Avenues), New York, NY 10011, 212.727.9400

See page 124 for details.

FULL MENU WITH VEGETARIAN AND VEGAN CHOICES

★★ / $$

28. Vegetarian Palate

258 Flatbush Avenue
(between Prospect Place and St. Mark's Avenue)
Park Slope, Brooklyn, NY 11217
718.623.8808

CHINESE

Hours:	Mon-Thu 11:30 a.m. to 11:00 p.m.
	Fri-Sat 11:30 a.m. to midnight
	Sun noon to 11:00 p.m.
Payment:	Credit cards
Alcohol:	No
Atmosphere:	Casual dining

It appears that Vegetarian Palate has built up a nice
following. Backlit stained glass adorning the walls and
the clean and relaxing decor make for a nice refuge
from the chaos of Flatbush Avenue. Unlike the other
veggie-friendly Chinese restaurants in the area, every-
thing on the menu is meatless, with at least several
dozen offerings. Think of the food here as Chinese with
a twist. Sugar Cane Drumsticks are cleverly shaped to
look like the real thing and served with Thai-style
sweet-chile sauce. Nobu Chicken Teriyaki is made from
battered and deep-fried taro-root chunks instead of the
typical soy protein or wheat-gluten chunks served else-
where. Peking Spare Ribs are another good choice.
Consider yourself lucky if you live in the vicinity of
Vegetarian Palate—if only all vegetarians had access to
takeout like this. Main dishes from $6 to $11.

VEGAN

★★★ / $

29. Veggie Castle

2242 Church Avenue
(between Bedford and Flatbush Avenues)
Flatbush, Brooklyn, NY 11226
718.703.1275

CARIBBEAN

Hours:	Sun-Thu 11:00 a.m. to 10:00 p.m.
	Fri-Sat 11:00 a.m. to 11:00 p.m.
Payment:	Cash only
Alcohol:	No
Atmosphere:	Counter service with casual seating

It seems appropriate that the king of the Brooklyn
Caribbean restaurants should be one called Veggie
Castle. Ironically converted from an old White Castle

restaurant, stepping into Veggie Castle is like being transported to a suburban burger joint, circa 1975, and that's part of its unique charm. That also means, unlike many Brooklyn Caribbean restaurants, there's plenty of seating available for dining in. Once you choose a tray size, the server will stuff it to capacity with boldly flavored meatless treats like Barbecue Chunks, Soy Mince Meat Loaf, Brown Stew Baked Tofu, Spiced Okra, and Collard Greens. Dairy-free pastries are offered as well, all made with whole-wheat flour, and the tart-like cookies are sweet and crispy. Strolling around the neighborhood after dark isn't advisable, but a lunch hour trip to Veggie Castle is very highly recommended. Combo plates $6 to $10.

VEGAN

★★ / $

30. Viva Natural Pizzeria (aka Cafe Viva)

1802 Avenue M
(at East 18th Street)
Midwood, Brooklyn, NY 11230
718.787.0050

ITALIAN, PIZZERIA

Hours:	Sun-Thu 11:00 a.m. to 11:00 p.m.
	Fri 11:00 a.m. to 3:00 p.m.
	Sat 6:30 p.m. to 1:00 a.m.
Payment:	Credit cards
Alcohol:	No
Atmosphere:	Counter service with casual seating

Other locations:

64 East 34th Street (between Park and Madison Avenues), New York, NY 10016, 212.779.4350;

Cafe Viva, 2578 Broadway (between West 97th and West 98th Streets), New York, NY 10025, 212.663.8482

See page 131 for details.

KOSHER VEGETARIAN WITH VEGAN CHOICES

★★★ / $

31. Waterfalls Cafe

144 Atlantic Avenue
(between Clinton and Henry Streets)
Brooklyn, NY 11201
718.488.8886; www.waterfallscafe.com

MIDDLE EASTERN

Hours:	noon to 10:30 p.m.
Payment:	Credit cards
Alcohol:	No
Atmosphere:	Casual dining

Several train lines stop nearby, and it's a quick ride on the F train from Manhattan to the Bergen Street stop, so you owe it to yourself to venture out to this strip of Atlantic Avenue. Middle Eastern restaurants, markets, and bakeries line the blocks, all with much to offer vegetarians. Start your visit with lunch at Waterfalls Café. The menu can be a bit overwhelming for novices, so the best advice is to arrive very hungry and order the vegetarian special platter. It's a huge plate (enough for two people, really) with samplings of every meatless item on the menu. Whatever you think you know about babaghanouj, you should forget. The deep, roasted flavor of the eggplant here is going to amaze you, even if you thought you didn't like babaghanouj. The falafel, cauliflower, tabouleh, and cracked wheat with lentils are also sure to impress. Sandwiches and main dishes from $6 to $8.

**FULL MENU WITH VEGETARIAN
AND VEGAN CHOICES**

Queens

★★ / $$

1. Annam Brahma

84-43 164th Street
(between 84th Drive and 84th Road)
Jamaica, Queens, NY 11432
718.523.2600

MULTIETHNIC

Hours:	Mon-Fri 11:00 a.m. to 10:00 p.m.
	Wed 11:00 a.m. to 4:00 p.m.
	Sun noon to 10:00 p.m.
Payment:	Cash only
Alcohol:	No
Atmosphere:	Casual dining

Like nearby Smile of the Beyond and Oneness Fountain Heart, this Jamaica restaurant is owned by students of spiritual leader Sri Chimnoy and located not too far from the Parsons Boulevard subway stop. Unlike the others and despite its quaint appearance from the outside, Annam Brahma is plastered with photographs of Chimnoy's accomplishments, and has publications, CDs, and post-cards for sale—all of which seem out of place at best. When first opened thirty years ago, Annam was an Indian restaurant. Things have changed for the worse. Not that the food is bad, but much of it is simply ordinary and nowhere near the level of the amazing Oneness Fountain Heart. Stick with the curries and the tasty Eggplant Parmigiana to be safe. But you're on your own if you want to experiment with Chinese stir-fries, veggie burgers, salads, and steamed vegetables. Main dishes from $5 to $7.

VEGETARIAN WITH VEGAN CHOICES

★★ / $$$

2. Baluchi's

113-30 76th Road (at Queens Boulevard)
Forest Hills, Queens, NY 11375
718.520.8600; www.baluchis.com

INDIAN

Hours:	Daily noon to 11:00 p.m.
Payment:	Cash only
Alcohol:	Beer and wine
Atmosphere:	Casual dining

Other locations:

All over Manhattan; see website.

See page 26 for details.

**FULL MENU WITH VEGETARIAN
AND VEGAN CHOICES**

★★★★ / $$

3. Buddha Bodai

42-96 Main Street (at Cherry Avenue)
Flushing, Queens, NY 11355
718.939.1188

CHINESE

Hours:	Mon-Fri 11:00 a.m. to 11:00 p.m.
	Sat-Sun 10:30 a.m. to 11:00 p.m.
Payment:	Credit cards
Alcohol:	No
Atmosphere:	Casual dining

Just a fifteen-minute walk south from the last stop on
the number 7 train and steps away from the Queens
Botanical Garden, Buddha Bodai should be a trip
required for all NYC vegetarians. This Chinese food sets
the standard by which all others are judged. Prices may
seem high for the neighborhood, but it's worth every
penny. Don't be confused by the dish names on the
epic menu ("pork," "fish," "duck," "lamb," "chicken"),
because everything here is meatless. Attention to detail
and the quality of the preparation of dishes like Sliced
Vegetarian Pork with Peking Sauce are astounding.
Your waiter will "fillet" the oddly named A. Sam Veg
Fish at tableside for a bit of drama. It's wrapped in sea-
weed and bean curd, served atop a bold and sophisti-
cated sweet-and-sour curry-like sauce. It may be a long
trip to Buddha Bodai from downtown Manhattan, but
it's totally worthwhile. Main dishes from $8 to $15.

KOSHER VEGETARIAN WITH VEGAN CHOICES

★★★ / $

4. Dimple

35-68 73rd Street
(between 35th and 37th Avenues)
Jackson Heights, Queens, NY 11372
718.458.8144

INDIAN

Hours:	Mon-Fri 9:00 a.m. to 10:00 p.m.
	Sat-Sun 11:00 a.m. to 10:00 p.m.
Payment:	Cash only
Alcohol:	No
Atmosphere:	Counter service with casual seating

Unlike the mostly "mild" Indian menus over on Lexington
Avenue, Dimple is a treat for vegetarians who prefer to
walk on the spicy side. Just hop on the E or F trains and
ride to the Roosevelt Avenue stop in Jackson Heights,
and then it's a short walk to Dimple. You'll have to ignore
the decor completely and help yourself to utensils,

napkins, and cups. Dimple, however, is serving up some of the best and most affordable southern Indian food in the city. The unique, pancake-like cheese dosas are a special treat. Other restaurants claim that their food is prepared fresh daily, but this is one of the only places in town where you can really taste the spinach in the Palak Paneer. Order plenty of bread and keep the yogurt raita close at hand to temper the spiciness—you're going to need it. At these prices, invite a bunch of friends along as well. Main dishes from $5 to $8.

**KOSHER FULL MENU WITH VEGETARIAN
AND VEGAN CHOICES**

★★★ / $

5. Dosa Diner

35-66 73rd Street (at 37th Avenue)
Jackson Heights, Queens, NY 11372
718.205.2218

INDIAN

Hours:	11:30 a.m. to 10:00 p.m.
Payment:	Cash only
Alcohol:	Full bar
Atmosphere:	Casual dining

In the space once occupied by the now legendary Anand Bhavan is this strictly vegetarian Southern Indian restaurant specializing in, as the name implies, dosas. This has become a crowded category with restaurants serving up these pancakes in Indian neighborhoods all over the city, but Dosa Diner is definitely one of the best. Like most ethnic restaurants outside of Manhattan, the food is a bit spicier than you might be used to, but don't let that scare you away. The decor leaves much to be desired as well, but a trip to bustling Jackson Heights is recommended. The enormous dosas are perfectly crispy with an ample amount of filling for scooping and dipping in cilantro chutney, and the soft uthappams are equally enjoyable. The idli and vada appetizers are some of the best you'll ever try, so bring some friends, order a little bit of everything to try, and prepare to be amazed at how little the meal costs when the check comes. Main dishes $4 to $5.

VEGETARIAN WITH VEGAN CHOICES

★★★ / $

6. Dosa Hutt

45-63 Bowne Street (at Holly Street)
Flushing, Queens, NY 11355
718.951.5897

INDIAN

Hours:	*Daily 10:00 a.m. to 9:00 p.m.*
Payment:	*Cash only*
Alcohol:	*No*
Atmosphere:	*Take-out service with casual seating*

Unless you happen to live in Flushing, it's quite a trip to get to Dosa Hutt, about 1.5 miles south of the Main Street subway station. Though a mostly residential block, it's probably not the best neighborhood to be wandering around in after dark. Despite those reservations, venturing to Dosa Hutt for lunch with a group of friends is highly recommended. Keep in mind that nobody comes here for the decor. A strictly vegetarian menu of filled pancake-style dosas and uthappams for dirt-cheap prices is the draw. If you've been disappointed by the mildly spiced dosas served elsewhere, you're in for a pleasant surprise. The Mysore Masala Dosa packs quite a punch, so be sure to order a mango lassi to cool things down. Appetizers like idly and medhu vada are served, but they're not quite up to par with the fantastic dosas. Don't expect any curry dishes here either. They do dosas (really well), and that's about it. Dosas from $3 to $5.

VEGETARIAN WITH VEGAN CHOICES

★★ / $$

7. Happy Buddha

135-37 37th Avenue
Flushing, Queens, NY 11354
718.358.0079; www.happybuddha.com

CHINESE

Hours:	*Sun-Thu 11:00 a.m. to 10:00 p.m.*
	Fri-Sat 11:00 a.m. to 11:00 p.m.
Payment:	*Credit cards*
Alcohol:	*No*
Atmosphere:	*Casual dining*

This Flushing restaurant, just a couple of blocks from the last stop on the number 7 train, was legendary among vegetarians when it shut down for extensive renovations. Now up and running again, Happy Buddha doesn't live up to its reputation. The modern decor, depending on your personal tastes, is a bit sterile. Though the menu is extensive (if perhaps a bit pricey), many of the dishes are confusing at best. The Crab Cakes appetizer is an oddity, both in terms of texture and flavor. The jellyfish appetizer, Summer in Hawaii, tastes even stranger than it sounds. Many of the entrées are interesting to behold, but just mediocre to taste. There is little doubt that this food is healthful, but you may be disappointed if you're more interested in flavor. And with the absolutely incredible Buddha Bodai located not too far away, it's hard to imagine why you'd ever visit Happy Buddha again. Entrees from $7 to $14.

KOSHER VEGETARIAN WITH VEGAN CHOICES

★★★ / $

8. I'Qulah

164-07 89th Avenue (at 164th Street)
Jamaica, Queens, NY 11432
718.523.4636

CARIBBEAN

Hours:	*Daily 7:00 a.m. to 10:00 p.m.*
Payment:	*Cash only*
Alcohol:	*No*
Atmosphere:	*Take-out service with casual seating*

I'Qulah's self-declared mission is to "tempt meat lovers" with well-prepared meat substitutes, including veggie goat, veggie chicken, and veggie beef stew, and they're doing a great job of it. Don't let the Plexiglas at the counter scare you away. It's a short walk from the 169th Street stop on the F train, and unlike many Caribbean restaurants in the boroughs, ample seating is available. A small-size combination platter is actually quite large, packed with an assortment of curries, vegetables, and rice, but don't be surprised if the staff offers you some more vegetables if you come close to emptying your plate. As if the curries aren't good enough, the veggie patties really stand out. Served hot, the crust is tender and flaky. You can't get better patties than this anywhere in New York City. If you order a ginger-spiked sorrel juice, be warned that it's not for the faint of heart. Combo plates from $6 to $10.

VEGAN WITH SEAFOOD CHOICES

★★ / $$

9. Jackson Diner

> 34-47 74th Street
> (between 34th and 35th Avenues)
> Jackson Heights, Queens, NY 11372
> 718.672.1232

INDIAN

Hours:	Sun-Thu 11:30 a.m. to 10:00 p.m.
	Fri-Sat 11:30 a.m. to 10:30 p.m.
Payment:	Cash only
Alcohol:	Full bar
Atmosphere:	Stylish casual dining

Just a half block from the Roosevelt Avenue station, Jackson Diner is conveniently located for Manhattanites not familiar with the neighborhood. The decor will also make you feel at home—it's bold and trendy and not like anything you'd expect while walking along busy 74th Street in Jackson Heights. Though the food might not be up to the level of nearby Dimple and Anand Bhavan, this is a good place to try with a group of friends. While the à la carte menu is pricey when compared even with Manhattan Indian restaurants, you can always come for lunch for the all-you-can-eat buffet, a remarkable bargain with ample meatless choices. Even with a refreshing mango lassi, your tab will still be under $10 per person. Malai Kofta (vegetable balls in a creamy sauce) and Navrattan Korma (mixed vegetables in a mild sauce), like all of the curries, are reliably tasty and satisfying. Main dishes from $9 to $10.

**FULL MENU WITH VEGETARIAN
AND VEGAN CHOICES**

★★ / $

10. Linda's Organic Kitchen and Market

> 81-22 Lefferts Boulevard
> (between Austin Street and 83rd Avenue)
> Kew Gardens, Queens, NY 11415
> 718.847.2233; www.lindasorganic.com

MULTIETHNIC, AMERICAN

Hours:	Mon-Tue, Thu-Fri,
	10:00 a.m. to 7:00 p.m.
	Wed 10:00 a.m. to 8:00 p.m.
	Sat 10:00 a.m. to 6:00 p.m.
	Sun 11:00 a.m. to 5:30 p.m.
Payment:	Credit cards
Alcohol:	No
Atmosphere:	Market with counter service and
	very limited seating

Strolling from the Union Turnpike subway station to Linda's along tree-lined Austin Avenue is a pleasure. Kew Gardens has some of the most gorgeous homes anywhere in the city. Though it's popular among locals in the know, casual passersby might not even notice that this well-stocked natural foods market offers organic prepared food, and that would be a shame. All manner of heartwarming veggie casseroles are sold by the pound, from Shepherd's Pie to dairy-free Macaroni and Cheese. Serve the veggie Franks and Beans to your kids and see if they miss the meat. Daily soup specials are offered as well, not to mention tofu burgers and meatballs, cold salads, burritos, wheat-free pizzas, and even vegan desserts. Add to that the friendly service and you have a winner for stopping by on the way home after work for a healthy meal. Main dishes sold by weight, from $3 to $6 on average.

VEGETARIAN WITH VEGAN CHOICES

★★ / $

11. Maharaja Quality Sweets & Snacks

73-10 37th Avenue
(between 73rd and 74th Streets)
Jackson Heights, Queens, NY 11372
718.505.2680

INDIAN

Hours:	Daily 10:00 a.m. to 10:00 p.m.
Payment:	Credit cards
Alcohol:	No
Atmosphere:	Casual dining

If you don't mind wandering a bit through Jackson Heights, Maharaja is located just off the busy 74th Street Indian strip and not too far from the Roosevelt Avenue subway station. Prepare to be amazed by the selection of sweets when you first walk in—you may not even notice that there is a strictly vegetarian Indian restaurant in the back. The desserts, in a wide variety of colors and flavors, are the highlight, so be sure to order an assortment box before you go. Bright lights and mirrored walls detract a bit from the dining experience, and there isn't a lot of seating, but at least it's clean. The $5 lunch buffet (including bread) is one of the best bargains you'll find anywhere. Many of the dishes taste even better than the famous Jackson Diner around the corner. Just try a little of everything, including paneers, kormas, and more. Main dishes from $6 to $7.

VEGETARIAN WITH VEGAN CHOICES

★★★ / $$

12. The Oneness Fountain Heart Restaurant

157-19 72nd Avenue (at Parsons Boulevard)
Flushing, Queens, NY 11367
718.591.3663

MULTIETHNIC

Hours:	Thu-Tue 11:30 a.m. to 9:00 p.m.
	Closed Wed
Payment:	Credit cards
Alcohol:	No
Atmosphere:	Casual dining

Even for the truly adventurous vegetarian, Oneness Fountain Heart is a long walk from the F train at Parsons Boulevard; driving is strongly recommended because this restaurant is too good to pass up. Tranquil running fountains, soothing music, plants all around, and pretty pale blue colors set the mood. If you didn't know it was strictly vegetarian, the menu might confuse you a bit with listings for duck, lamb, chicken, and burgers. Start off with a salad like the stunning Spring Chicken, featuring Cajun-grilled strips of veggie chicken over fresh greens and toasted walnuts, topped with a fantastic mango-lime dressing. Entrées are entirely satisfying. Golden Lamb is a sumptuous mound of veggie lamb, onions, and rice, covered with smoky grilled mozzarella. If you can't bear to eat even one more bite, order a slice of the divine vegan chocolate cake to go. Main dishes from $8 to $10.

VEGETARIAN WITH VEGAN CHOICES

★★★ / $

13. Shamiana

42-47 Main Street
(between Franklin and Blossom Streets)
Flushing, Queens, NY 11355
718.539.0042

INDIAN

Hours:	Daily 10:30 a.m. to 9:00 p.m.
Payment:	Cash only
Alcohol:	No
Atmosphere:	Takeout with casual seating

Not far from the last stop on the number 7 train, Shamiana is situated on a small strip of Indian shops in Flushing's Chinatown district and doubles as a sweets and snack shop, offering brightly colored treats. Communicating with the staff isn't easy, so if you're curious about the desserts, just point to whatever catches your eye. Many of the sweets are perfect for cooling things down, and you're going to need it. Forget about the mildly spiced Indian fare you've tried in Manhattan. The Mysore Masala Dosa packs quite a punch. Even the Matar Paneer (peas and cheese) is laced with whole dried chiles. If you like your food on the spicy side, Shamiana is definitely worth a try. Just don't expect much in the way of decor, and keep your valuables close by. If you've never been to Flushing before, come for lunch with friends, just to be safe. Main dishes from $5 to $7.

VEGETARIAN WITH VEGAN CHOICES

★★★★ / $

14. Singh's Roti Shop and Bar

131 Liberty Avenue
(between 131st and 132nd Streets)
Richmond Hill, Queens, NY 11419
718.323.5990

CARIBBEAN

Hours:	*Daily 6:00 a.m. to midnight*
Payment:	*Cash only*
Alcohol:	*Full bar*
Atmosphere:	*Counter service with casual seating*

When you have some time to spare, take the A train all the way out to Lefferts Boulevard and walk about ten blocks east to find Singh's. Keep walking past all the other roti shops along Liberty Avenue and you won't regret it. Despite the meat offerings, Singh's is a vegetarian's paradise. Get ready for the best roti (a giant, warm flat bread) you'll ever try, with rich, yet simply prepared fillings like mashed pumpkin and pureed spinach. The spinach is as good or better than any Saag you've had in even the city's best Indian restaurants. And don't leave without trying a "double": two small, warm and puffy flat breads are served sandwich style with a curried chickpea filling and three different hot sauces. Ask for a Trinidadian soda to complete the meal, and if you're not too stuffed, try a piece of the "fudge" as well. Main dishes $3 to $5.

FULL MENU WITH VEGETARIAN
AND VEGAN CHOICES

★★ / $

15. Smile of the Beyond

86-14 Parsons Boulevard (at 86th Avenue)
Jamaica, Queens, NY 11432
718.739.7453

MULTIETHNIC, AMERICAN

Hours:	Mon-Fri 7:00 a.m. to 4:00 p.m.
	Sat 7:00 a.m. to 3:00 p.m.
	Closed Sun
Payment:	Cash only
Alcohol:	No
Atmosphere:	Casual dining

Don't worry if you don't know your way around Queens.
Smile of the Beyond is just a block or two up the hill
from the Parsons Boulevard stop on the F train,
although from the looks of this restaurant, you'll feel as
if you've stepped into a country diner in rural
Massachusetts. Lunch hour is a madhouse at Smile, and
the waitstaff is pushed to its limits. Bring your patience
with you and plan to wait a while for your order.
Fortunately most of the food is worth it. A little experi-
mentation may be required, because the Steak Burger
isn't nearly as good as it sounds. On the other hand, the
open-faced hot mushroom sandwich is comfort food at
its best. The zesty Mexican Tacos with veggie chili are
another winner. A complete breakfast menu is offered
for early morning diners, including omelets, oatmeal,
pancakes, and more. Just don't forget to order a side of
veggie bacon with that. Main dishes from $5 to $7.

VEGETARIAN WITH VEGAN CHOICES

★★ / $

16. Sybil's Bakery & Restaurant

159-24 Hillside Avenue (at 160th Street)
Jamaica, Queens, NY 11432
718.297.2359

CARIBBEAN, BAKERY

Hours:	Mon-Thu 8:00 a.m. to 10:00 p.m.
	Fri-Sat 8:00 a.m. to 11:00 p.m.
	Sun 10:00 a.m. to 10:00 p.m.
Payment:	Cash only
Alcohol:	No
Atmosphere:	Counter service with casual seating

Other locations:
132-17 Liberty Avenue (at 133rd Street), Richmond Hill,
Queens, NY 11419, 718.835.9235

Peek in the window of Sybil's (just steps from the
Parsons Boulevard subway station) and you'll spy an

array of meatless hot buffet offerings. Walk inside, and it's a different story. As the name implies, Sybil's is first and foremost a bakery. Specializing in Guyanese desserts, there's a good chance you've never seen sweets like this before: dense fruitcakes with thick icing, coconut rolls (like a roulade), cassava pone, coconut drops, and more. There turns out to be loads of meat offerings as well, but don't let that scare you away. Order a meatless combo plate, and prepare to be satisfied. Choose from curried vegetables, veggie lo mein, fried plantains, curried chickpeas, and the delightfully chunky pureed pumpkin. Another peculiar treat are the donut hole–like fritters, sold in a bag with a container of "pickle sauce." Dunk and enjoy. Friendly service completes this unique experience. Combo plates from $6 to $10.

FULL MENU WITH VEGETARIAN
AND VEGAN CHOICES

★★★ / $$

17. Zen Pavilion

251-15 Northern Boulevard
(between Little Neck and Marathon Parkways)
Little Neck, Queens, NY 11362
718.281.1500

CHINESE

Hours:	Sun-Thu 11:30 a.m. to 10:00 p.m.
	Fri-Sat 11:30 a.m. to 11:00 p.m.
Payment:	Credit cards
Alcohol:	No
Atmosphere:	Casual to mid-scale dining

Though it may be several miles from the nearest subway station at the easternmost edge of Queens, Zen Pavilion is definitely worth the trip. In both its vast size and the slightly elegant decor, the Pavilion resembles the banquet halls of Chinatown. Yet even on a Saturday night you won't feel out of place in a pair of jeans. Convincing meat-like dishes dominate the strictly vegetarian appetizers, including the Boneless BBQ Ribs, possibly the best anywhere in the city. Dim sum and sushi are available as well, and you really can't go wrong with the entrées. Sizzling Sensation (crispy wheat gluten in an orange-flavored brown sauce) is transferred to a hot plate at tableside; the sound of the simmering sauce turns heads from across the dining room. Fisherman Delight is cleverly formed to resemble a real fish and served with a tasty, sweet sauce. Main dishes from $8 to $14.

KOSHER VEGETARIAN WITH VEGAN CHOICES

★★★ / $$

1. H.I.M. Royal

2130 White Plains Road (at Lydig Avenue)
Bronx, NY 10462
718.239.7146

CARIBBEAN

Hours:	Mon-Sat 8:00 a.m. to 9:00 p.m. Closed Sun
Payment:	Cash only
Alcohol:	No
Atmosphere:	Counter service with limited bar stool seating

It looks like the Bronx is batting a thousand in more ways than one. H.I.M. may be the only Bronx restaurant in this guidebook, but it turns out to be a winner. Yes, it's a long trip on the number 2 train from downtown Manhattan to the Pelham Parkway subway stop, but at least it's just a one-block walk to the restaurant from there, and bar stool seating is available, so you won't have to take your order to go. Like most vegan Caribbean joints, for the best experience try ordering a combination plate. For $9 you can get a little of everything available (menu options vary daily), and the Veggie Chicken and Curry Tofu are so good, you may find yourself asking for seconds. Fried plantains, rice, and greens round out the meal, with a deliciously sweet pancake atop every platter. If your sweet tooth still needs satisfying, try a slice of the vegan Peach Cake. Combo platters $5 to $9.

VEGAN

Greenmarkets

Manhattan

Abingdon Square
  West 12th Street and Hudson Street
  Sat 8:00 a.m. to 1:00 p.m.
  Year-round

Audobon Terrace
  West 155th Street at Broadway
  Sat 8:00 a.m. to 2:00 p.m.
  Jul–Nov

Bowling Green
  Broadway and Battery Place
  Tue & Thu 8:00 a.m. to 5:00 p.m.
  Year-round

Columbia
  Broadway between West 114th and West 115th Streets
  Thu 8:00 a.m. to 6:00 p.m.
  Year-round
  Sun 8:00 a.m. to 6:00 p.m.
  May–Dec

Dag Hammarskjold Plaza
  East 47th Street and Second Avenue
  Wed 8:00 a.m. to 6:00 p.m.
  Year-round

Downtown Path Station
  Church and Vesey Streets at World Trade Center Train Station
  Tue 8:00 a.m. to 6:00 p.m.
  Apr–Dec
  Thu 8:00 a.m. to 6:00 p.m.
  Jun–Dec

57th Street
  West 57th Street and Ninth Avenue
  Wed & Sat 8:00 a.m. to 6:00 p.m.
  Year-round

Inwood
  Isham Street at Seaman and Cooper Streets
  Sat 8:00 a.m. to 3:00 p.m.
  Jun–Nov

Murray Hill
  Second Avenue at 33rd Street
  Sat 8:00 a.m. to 3:00 p.m.
  Jul–Nov

97th Street
  Columbus Avenue at West 97th Street
  Fri 8:00 a.m. to 2:00 p.m.
  Year-round

175th Street
  West 175th Street and Broadway
  Thursday 8:00 a.m. to 6:00 p.m.
  Jun–Nov

Rockefeller Center
  Rockefeller Plaza at West 50th Street
  Thu, Fri & Sat 8:00 a.m. to 6:00 p.m.
  Jul–Aug

77th Street—I.S. 44
  West 77th Street and Columbus Avenue
  Sun 10:00 a.m. to 5:00 p.m.
  Year-round

South Street Seaport
Fulton Street (between Walter and Pearl Streets)
Fri 8:00 a.m. to 5:00 p.m.
Jun–Nov

St. Mark's Church
East 10th Street and Second Avenue
Tue 8:00 a.m. to 7:00 p.m.
May–Dec

Stranger's Gate
West 106th Street and Central Park West
Sat 8:00 a.m. to 3:00 p.m.
Jul–Nov

Tompkins Square
East 7th Street and Avenue A
Sun 9:00 a.m. to 6:00 p.m.
Year-round

Tribeca
Greenwich Street (between Chambers and Duane Streets)
Wed & Sat 8:00 a.m. to 3:00 p.m.
Year-round

Tucker Square
Columbus Avenue (between West 65th and West 66th Streets)
Thu & Sat 8:00 a.m. to 5:00 p.m.
Year-round

Union Square
East 17th Street and Broadway
Mon, Wed, Fri, Sat 8:00 a.m. to 6:00 p.m.
Year-round

The Wagner Houses
East 120th Street at First Avenue
Thu 8:00 a.m. to 5:00 p.m.
Jul–Nov

Brooklyn

Bedford-Stuyvesant
Fulton Street (between Stuyvesant and Utica Avenues)
Sat 8:00 a.m. to 3:00 p.m.
Jul–Oct

Borough Hall
Court and Remsen Streets
Tue, Thu, Sat 8:00 a.m. to 6:00 p.m.
Tue & Sat Year-round
Thu Apr–Dec

Borough Park
14th Avenue (between 49th and 50th Streets)
Thu 8:00 a.m. to 3:00 p.m.
Jul–Oct

Cortelyou
Cortelyou Road (between Argyle and Rugby Roads)
Sat 8:00 a.m. to 6:00 p.m.
Jul–Nov

Fort Green
Washington Park (between Dekalb and Willoughby Streets)
Sat 8:00 a.m. to 5:00 p.m.
Jul–Dec

Grand Army Plaza
NW entrance to Prospect Park
Sat 8:00 a.m. to 4:00 p.m.
Year-round

Greenpoint—McCarren Park
Lorimer Street and Driggs Avenue
Sat 8:00 a.m. to 3:00 p.m.
Year-round

Sunset Park
4th Avenue (between 59th and 60th Streets)
Sat 8:00 a.m. to 3:00 p.m.
Jul–Oct

Williamsburg
Havemeyer Street and Broadway
Thu 8:00 a.m. to 5:00 p.m.
Jul–Oct

Windsor Terrace
Prospect Park West and 15th Street
Wed 8:00 a.m. to 3:00 p.m.
Jun–Nov

Queens

Astoria
31st Avenue between 12th and 14th Streets
Wed 8:00 a.m. to 5:00 p.m.
Jul–Nov

Atlas Park
Cooper Avenue and 80th Street
Sat 8:00 a.m. to 3:00 p.m.
Jul–Nov

Jackson Heights
34th Avenue between 77th and 78th Streets
Sun 8:00 a.m. to 3:00 p.m.
May–Nov

Long Island City
48th Avenue at Vernon Boulevard
Sat 8:00 a.m. to 3:00 p.m.
Jul–Nov

Bronx

Lincoln Hospital
148th Street and Morris Avenue
South of hospital entrance
Tue & Fri 8:00 a.m. to 3:00 p.m.
Jul–Oct

Poe Park
Grand Concourse and 192nd Street
Tue 8:00 a.m. to 2:00 p.m.
Jul–Nov

Yankee Stadium
Grand Concourse and 161st Street
Tue 8:00 a.m. to 6:00 p.m.
Jun–Nov

Staten Island

St. George
Borough Hall parking lot
St. Mark's and Hyatt Streets
Sat 8:00 a.m. to 2:00 p.m.
May–Nov

Historic Richmond Town
441 Clark Avenue off Arthur Kill Road
Sat 8:00 a.m. to 3:00 p.m.
Jul–Nov

Natural Foods Markets, Green Grocers, and Food Co-ops

Manhattan

A Matter of Health
>1478 First Avenue (at East 77th Street)
>New York, NY 10021
>212.288.8280

Bell Bates Natural Food Market
>97 Reade Street (between Church Street and West Broadway)
>New York, NY 10013
>212.267.4300

Commodities Natural
>165 First Avenue (at East 10th Street)
>New York, NY 10003
>212.260.2600

Earthmatters
>177 Ludlow Street (between Houston and Stanton Streets)
>New York, NY 10022
>212.475.4180
>www.earthmatters.com

Fairway
>2127 Broadway (at West 74th Street)
>New York, NY 10023
>212.595.1888

Fairway
>2328 Twelfth Avenue (between West 132nd and West 133rd Streets)
>New York, NY 10027
>212.234.3883

4th Street Food Co-op
>48 East 4th Street (between Second Avenue and the Bowery)
>New York, NY 10003
>212.674.3623
>www.4thstreetfoodcoop.com

Health & Harmony
>470 Hudson Street (between Barrow & Grove Streets)
>New York, NY 10014
>212.691.3036

Healthfully Organic Market
>98 East 4th Street (between First and Second Avenues)
>New York, NY 10003
>212.598.0777

Health Nuts
>1208 Second Avenue (at East 63rd Street)
>New York, NY 10021
>212.593.0116

Health Nuts
>835 Second Avenue (at East 45th Street)
>New York, NY 1017
>212.490.2979

Health Nuts
>2141 Broadway (at West 75th Street)
>New York, NY 10023
>212.724.1972

Health Nuts
2611 Broadway (at West 99th Street)
New York, NY 10025
212.678.0054

Healthy Chelsea
248 West 23rd Street (between Seventh and Eighth Avenues)
New York, NY 10011
212.691.0286

Healthy Pleasures Market
2493 Broadway (at West 93rd Street)
New York, NY 10025
212.787.6465

Integral Yoga Natural Foods
229 West 13th Street (between Seventh and Eighth Avenues)
New York, NY 10013
212.243.2642
www.iynaturalfoods.com

LifeThyme Market
410 Sixth Avenue (between West 8th and West 9th Streets)
New York, NY 10011
212.420.9099

LifeThyme Market
2275 Broadway (at West 82nd Street)
New York, NY 10024
212.721.9000

Manhattan Fruit Exchange
Chelsea Market Building
75 Ninth Avenue (at West 15th Street)
New York, NY 10011
212.989.2444

May Wah Healthy Vegetarian Food
213 Hester Street (at Baxter Street)
New York, NY 10013
212.334.4428

Natural Frontier
1424 Third Avenue (between East 80th and East 81st Streets)
New York, NY 10028
212.794.0922
www.naturalfrontiermarket.com

Natural Frontier
266 Third Avenue (between East 21st and East 22nd Streets)
New York, NY 10010
212.228.9133
www.naturalfrontiermarket.com

Prana Foods
125 First Avenue (between East 7th Street and St. Mark's Place)
New York, NY 10003
212.982.7306

VegeCyber
210 Centre Street (between Canal and Grand Streets)
New York, NY 10013
212.625.3980
www.vegecyber.com

Westerly Natural Market
913 Eighth Avenue (between West 54th and West 55th Streets)
New York, NY 10019
212.586.5262
www.westerlynaturalmarket.com

Whole Foods Market
250 Seventh Avenue (at West 24th Street)
New York, NY 10001
212.294.5969
www.wholefoodsmarket.com

Whole Foods Market
10 Columbus Circle (near East 59th Street and Broadway)
New York, NY 10019
212.823.9600

Whole Foods Market
4 Union Square South (between Broadway and University Place),
New York, NY 10003
212.673.5388

Whole Foods Market
Greenwich Street and Warren Street
New York, NY

Whole Foods Market
Bowery and Houston Street
New York, NY

Whole Body at Whole Foods Market
260 Seventh Avenue (at West 25th Street)
New York, NY 10001
212.924.9972
www.wholefoodsmarket.com

Wild Oats Uptown Whole Foods
2421 Broadway (at West 89th Street)
New York, NY 10024
212.874.4000
www.wildoats.com

Brooklyn

Back to the Land
142 Seventh Avenue (between Carroll Street and Garfield Place)
Park Slope, Brooklyn, NY 11215
718.768.5564

Flatbush Food Co-op
1318 Corelyou Road (between Rugby and Argyle Roads)
Flatbush, Brooklyn, NY 11226
718.284.9717
www.flatbushfoodcoop.com

Imhotep's
734 Nostrand Avenue (between Park and Prospect Places)
Crown Heights, Brooklyn, NY 11216
718.493.2395

Park Health Foods
247 Union Street (between Clinton and Court Streets)
Park Slope, Brooklyn, NY 11231
718.802.1652

Park Slope Food Co-op
782 Union Street (between Sixth and Seventh Avenues)
Park Slope, Brooklyn, NY 11215
718.622.0560
www.parkslopefoodcoop.com

Perelandra Natural Food Center
175 Remsen Street (between Clinton and Court Streets)
Brooklyn Heights, Brooklyn, NY 11201
718.855.6068

Pumpkin's Organic Market
> 1302 Eighth Avenue (between 13th and 14th Streets)
> Park Slope, Brooklyn, NY 11215
> 718.499.8539

Whole Foods Market
> 220 3rd Street
> Brooklyn, NY

Queens

Health Nuts
> Bay Terrace Shopping Center
> 26th Avenue and Bell Boulevard
> Bayside, Queens, NY 11361
> 718.225.8164

Linda's Organic Kitchen and Market
> 81–22 Lefferts Boulevard (between Austin Street and 83rd
> Avenue)
> Kew Gardens, Queens, NY 11415
> 718.847.2233
> www.lindasorganic.com

Quantum Leap Natural Market
> 65–60 Fresh Meadow Lane (between 65th and 67th Avenues)
> Fresh Meadows, Queens, NY 11365
> 718.461.1307
> www.quantumleapnatural.com

Staten Island

Family Health Foods
> 7000 Amboy Road (between Bethel and Page Avenues)
> Tottenville, Staten Island, NY 10307
> 718.967.9674
> www.familyhealthfoods.com

Family Health Foods
> 177 New Dorp Lane (between 8th and 9th Streets)
> New Dorp, Staten Island, NY 10306
> 718.351.7004
> www.familyhealthfoods.com

Family Health Foods
> 1789 Victory Boulevard (at Manor Road)
> Westerleigh, Staten Island, NY 10314
> 718.422.0357
> www.familyhealthfoods.com

Tastebud's Natural Foods
> 1807 Hylan Boulevard (at Buel Avenue)
> Dongan Hills, Staten Island, NY 10305
> 718.351.8693

Bronx

Good 'n' Natural Health Food Market
> 2173 White Plains Road
> Bronx, NY 10462
> 718.931.4335

Resources

GREENMARKET
Council on the Environment of NYC
51 Chambers Street, Room 228
New York, NY 10007
212.788.7900
www.cenyc.org

NEW YORK NATURALLY:
COMMUNITY RESOURCE FOR NATURAL LIVING
Published by
City Spirit Natural Pages
7872 Sir Francis Drake Boulevard
P.O. Box 267
Lagunitas, CA 94938
800.486.4794

NEW YORK SPIRIT (magazine)
107 Sterling Place
Brooklyn, NY 11217
800.634.0989
718.638.3733
www.nyspirit.com

THE NEW YORK OPEN CENTER
83 Spring Street
New York, NY 10012
Registration desk: 212.219.2527 x110
Holistic education and wellness services

SATYA (magazine)
539 1st Street
Brooklyn, NY 11215
718.832.9557
www.satyamag.com

"VEGAN RESTAURANT GUIDE TO NEW YORK CITY 2003"
(pamphlet)
Published by
The Friends of Animals
1841 Broadway, Suite 812
New York, NY 10023
212.247.8120
www.friendsofanimals.org

ALPHABETICAL INDEX

CUISINE INDEX

NEIGHBORHOOD INDEX

GRAMERCY/FLATIRON DISTRICT

Top 10 Index

*The following top ten lists are
in alphabetical order.*

Top 10 for Food

1. Bloom
2. Buddha Bodai
3. Candle 79
4. Hangawi
5. Lupa
6. Pure Food and Wine
7. Red Bamboo Vegetarian Soul Café
8. Singh's Roti Shop and Bar
9. Tabla Bread Bar
10. Vatan

Top 10 for Atmosphere

1. Bloom
2. Candle 79
3. Franchia
4. Hangawi
5. Heirloom
6. Lupa
7. Peep
8. Pure Food and Wine
9. Red Bamboo Vegetarian Soul Café
10. Tabla Bread Bar

Top 10 Best Buys

1. Azuri Cafe
2. Dosa Diner
3. Dosa Hutt
4. 18 Arhans Restaurant
5. Miriam's
6. Pommes Frites
7. Pukk
8. Singh's Roti Shop and Bar
9. Sullivan Street Bakery
10. Veggie Castle

BUSINESS REPLY MAIL

FIRST CLASS MAIL   PERMIT NO 23   LAYTON, UT

POSTAGE WILL BE PAID BY THE ADDRESSEE

Veg Out
Vegetarian
Guide®
P.O. BOX 667
LAYTON, UT 84041

NO POSTAGE
NECESSARY
IF MAILED
IN THE
UNITED STATES

Veg Out
vegetarian Guide®

Your Name _____

Address _____

Phone Number _____

E-mail _____

Restaurant You Are Recommending

Name _____

Address _____

Phone Number _____

Recommended dishes _____

Comments _____
_____
_____
_____

If this restaurant is chosen for an upcoming edition of a VegOut! guide, you will receive a free copy of that guide.